D1118651

PROFILES

Amazing Archaeologists and Their Finds
America's Most Influential First Ladies
America's Third-Party Presidential Candidates
Black Abolitionists and Freedom Fighters
Black Civil Rights Champions
Charismatic Cult Leaders
Environmental Pioneers
Great Auto Makers and Their Cars
Great Justices of the Supreme Court
Hatemongers and Demagogues
Hoaxers and Hustlers
Influential Economists
International Terrorists
Journalists Who Made History
Legendary Labor Leaders
Philanthropists and Their Legacies
Spectacular Space Travelers
Top Entrepreneurs and Their Businesses
Top Lawyers and Their Famous Cases
Treacherous Traitors
Utopian Visionaries
Women Chosen for Public Office
Women in Medicine
Women Inventors and Their Discoveries
Women of Adventure
Women of the U.S. Congress
Women Who Led Nations
Women Who Reformed Politics
Women With Wings
The World's Greatest Explorers

WOMEN of ADVENTURE

Jacqueline McLean

The Oliver Press, Inc.
Minneapolis

*For my sister, an adventurous woman,
and for Bill, with whom life is an adventure
with love*

The author and publisher wish to thank **Mary Sanford McLean**
for the research and writing of Chapter 7.

Copyright © 2003 by The Oliver Press, Inc.
All rights reserved.
No part of this book may be reproduced in any form or by
any means without permission in writing from the publisher.
Please address inquiries to:

The Oliver Press, Inc.
Charlotte Square
5707 West 36th Street
Minneapolis, MN 55416-2510

Library of Congress Cataloging-in-Publication Data

McLean, Jacqueline.
   Women of adventure / Jacqueline McLean.
      p. cm. — (Profiles)
   Includes bibliographical references (p.).
   ISBN 1-881508-73-0
      1. Women adventurers—Biography—Juvenile literature.
   2. Women travelers—Biography—Juvenile literature. I. Title
   II. Profiles (Minneapolis, Minn.)

G200 .M355 2003
910'.82—dc21
[B]

                                                     2001059312

ISBN 1-881508-73-0
Printed in the United States of America
09 08 07 06 05 04 03   8 7 6 5 4 3 2 1

Contents

Introduction 7

Chapter 1   Mary Kingsley
             Victorian Voyager in Africa 17

Chapter 2   Alexandra David-Neel
             Pilgrim in Tibet 37

Chapter 3   Harriet Chalmers Adams
             In the Footsteps of the Conquistadors..57

Chapter 4   Marguerite Baker Harrison
             The Secret Agent from Baltimore.........75

Chapter 5   Louise Arner Boyd
             Arctic Pioneer 95

Chapter 6   Freya Stark
             Nomad in the Middle East 115

Chapter 7   Ann Bancroft
             To the Ends of the Earth 133

Bibliography 152

Index 154

LIBRARY
DEXTER SCHOOLS
DEXTER, NM 88230

aquesta carauana es partida de tiripi
de sarra pasar adlatayo

The tradition of European exploration was built on
the example of daring male adventurers such as
Marco Polo (1254-1324). His widely read book
about his journey along the silk road to China
remained the major source of information about many
parts of the Far East until the nineteenth century.

Introduction

"Tell me, Muse, of the man of many ways, who was driven [on] far journeys, after he had sacked Troy's sacred citadel. Many were they whose cities he saw, whose minds he learned of. . . ." These lines from the ancient Greek epic *The Odyssey* introduce the story of daring Odysseus, who ventured into uncharted lands and returned home as an old man after a lifetime of wandering. Meanwhile, his faithful wife, Penelope, remained at home; her tale was not one of adventure but of patience and quiet devotion. *The Odyssey* helped establish a standard that took centuries to erode. Men were supposed to be curious and brave, traveling far and wide to make war, trade goods, and discover what lay beyond the world they knew. Marco Polo, who journeyed overland from Italy to China and back again in the late thirteenth century; Christopher

Columbus, whose fifteenth-century voyages opened up the New World of the Americas; and Sir Francis Drake, who circumnavigated the globe in 1577—these were only a few of the European men who won fame with their adventures in strange lands and uncharted seas. Women, however, were expected to remain behind to bear and raise children and care for their homes. Until the eighteenth century, very few European women were free to travel outside their own countries or even towns.

Besides traditional domestic responsibilities, there were other reasons why women were not involved in early exploration. One was that they were not thought strong enough to endure the dangers of travel. Until the steamship and the railroad were invented in the 1700s, journeys were long and rigorous. It took Marco Polo, for instance, three years to return to Italy from China. Travel was also prohibitively costly. Explorers relied on wealthy patrons to fund their journeys; Columbus was sponsored by Queen Isabella and King Ferdinand of Spain, and Drake was backed by England's Queen Elizabeth I. Without money or property of their own and patrons willing to support them, most women could not afford to venture far from home. The few exceptions were women of the ruling classes, who had more money, more opportunities to travel, and servants to care for their homes and children in their absence. The French queen Eleanor of Aquitaine, for example, accompanied her husband and his crusading army on an overland journey to the Middle East in the 1100s.

In the eighteenth and nineteenth centuries, the trend in exploration shifted toward scientific and missionary expeditions. Having conquered and colonized many new territories, Europeans now sought to learn more about foreign geography, languages, and cultures. Geographical societies sponsored most major expeditions that recorded and studied details about other lands. Women, however, remained excluded from these organizations. England's Royal Geographical Society did not freely admit women until 1913, and the Explorers Club of New York still refused women as members as late as 1925.

By the mid-1800s, however, travel was much easier, cheaper, and more accessible for average people, and women could find ways around the lack of formal support. One way was to accompany their husbands or fathers on their travels. Lucy Atkinson, for example, journeyed by horse through remote areas of Siberia with her artist husband between 1848 and 1853, giving birth to a son along the way. Elizabeth Sarah Mazuchelli (1832-1914), also traveling with her husband, became the first European woman to penetrate the interior of the eastern Himalayas. Florence von Sass Baker (1841?-1916) and her husband explored Africa for nearly eight years, discovering Lake Albert, a source of the Nile River. Lady Anne Blunt (1837-1917) accompanied her husband on travels through

Anne Blunt published two books about her journeys through the uncharted desert by camel and horse.

the eastern Mediterranean region, spending two winters living among the Bedouin tribes of Arabia.

As more women gained access to higher education and professional work, they acquired some of the freedom and income they needed to realize their dreams of independent travel. One of the first and most famous solo female travelers was Englishwoman Isabella Lucy Bird Bishop (1831-1904). When a spinal operation left her an invalid at the age of 20, a doctor prescribed travel to help her grow strong again. Little did anyone know that this advice would launch a long career of adventure. Over the next 50 years, Bishop visited the United States, Canada, Hawaii, Australia, New Zealand, Japan, Korea, India,

Malaysia, Persia (now Iran), and Syria. Her travels and the nine books she published about them made her so popular and respected that she became one of the first women elected to the Royal Geographical Society. With her courage and independence, Bishop blazed a trail for future female explorers to follow.

In the century following Bishop's death, women ventured all over the world, from jungles to mountains to deserts to icy oceans, and their achievements were as diverse as the places they explored. Agnes Smith Lewis (1843-1926) and Margaret Smith Gibson (1843-1920),

Isabella Bishop took her first elephant ride while visiting Malaysia in 1878.

twin sisters, discovered a priceless ancient biblical manuscript in a remote Egyptian monastery. Delia Akeley (1875-1970) became the first woman to cross the continent of Africa and spent months living with the Pygmy people of the Congo. Violet Cressy-Marcks (1890?-1970) traveled around the world eight times. Ella Maillart (1903-1997) made a 3,500-mile journey across central Asia, and Dervla Murphy (b. 1931) bicycled alone from France to India. Traveling women hunted or photographed wild animals, collected plant specimens, climbed mountains, made maps, discovered artifacts from ancient civilizations, and studied the lives and customs of other cultures. They faced many obstacles, but they also had

On her four major African expeditions, Delia Akeley hunted elephants, crocodiles, and other wild animals for display in natural history museums across the United States.

unique advantages. Being able to speak freely with the women of other cultures, for example (when male explorers were often forbidden to do so), gave them access to previously unavailable information about the daily life of these societies. In both conventional and unconventional ways, women contributed significantly to exploration.

Women of Adventure profiles seven of the most famous and well-traveled women who explored the world in the nineteenth and twentieth centuries. Mary Kingsley left behind the rigid social restrictions of Victorian England for the wilds of West Africa, transforming herself into an expert on native culture. Alexandra David-Neel's passion for Eastern philosophy and religion led her to spend 14 years traveling throughout India, China, and Tibet. Harriet Chalmers Adams journeyed to every country in Latin America, then founded and led the Society of Woman Geographers—an organization to support female explorers and travelers. Another founding member of the society, Marguerite Baker Harrison, reported on conditions in post-World War I Germany and Russia as a spy for the U.S. government, enduring hardships that included nearly a year in prison. Louise Arner Boyd used her wealth to organize and lead scientific expeditions to the cold, remote regions around the North Pole, taking thousands of photographs that proved instrumental in creating accurate Arctic maps. A British scholar of Arabic and Persian as well as a best-selling author, Freya Stark spent years traveling the Middle East and became one of

On August 3, 1938, Louise Arner Boyd (center) landed farther north on the east coast of Greenland than any Arctic explorer ever had before.

the most honored explorers of the twentieth century. Ann Bancroft became the first woman to cross the ice to the North Pole, led the first women's expedition to the South Pole, and, in 2000-2001, was one of the first two women to cross Antarctica on foot. Her commitment to educate children about exploration and to support and publicize women's achievements has raised the possibility of an even greater role for women of adventure in the twenty-first century.

Women who have independently ventured far from home have had many different motivations. Some sought data for scientific and scholarly work, investigating language, history, religion, human cultures, or the natural world. Others wanted to chart the geography of lands not yet mapped. Some traveled for political reasons, critiquing or supporting their governments' roles abroad, and some for creative reasons, drawing or writing about the new lands that they visited. Others attempted to improve the quality of life in other countries by bringing religious ideas, health care, or modern technology. Many wanted freedom from social restrictions or the chance to prove that women could endure and achieve as much as men. And most, whether they admitted it or not, sought the newness of the unknown, the thrill of discovery, and the opportunity to test their strength.

Each of the women profiled here learned, along the way, to embrace her love of adventure and exploration. Ann Bancroft summed it up best: "When you're pulling a sled, there's not a whole lot to do with your mind all day long . . . [and] it struck me, *This feels so great. I love doing what I'm doing*. . . . As I was pulling my sled toward the South Pole, I thought, *Oh, I am supposed to be doing this. I've been thinking about this since I was a little girl and here I am pulling this sled*. I finally realized that what I was doing was what I was supposed to be doing all along. I'm a teacher, but I'm also an explorer. . . . My classroom is these trips, these faraway places."

While maintaining her image as a proper Victorian lady, Mary Kingsley (1862-1900) accomplished what few women or men of her time had ever attempted: venturing alone into West Africa to study its geography, wildlife, and people.

1

Mary Kingsley
Victorian Voyager in Africa

*I*n 1893, Mary Kingsley stood at the rail of a ship traveling south along the west coast of Africa, mesmerized by the scene before her. Unlike her native London with its buildings and bridges, West Africa seemed without any human imprint whatsoever. For as far as the eye could see stretched a band of pure white sand, a wall of dark, impenetrable forest, and the colorful sky. It was a landscape, Kingsley wrote, in which "you automatically believe that nothing else but this sort of world, past, present, or future can ever have existed: and that cities and mountains are but the memories of dreams." She found the sight incredibly beautiful, and long after her return to England, Africa continued to call to her. Kingsley voyaged to West Africa three times, making scientific observations and becoming an authority on indigenous (native) culture. What kept her coming back, however, was her enduring love for Africa's wild beauty and the freedom she felt there. Experiencing Africa, she wrote, "takes all the color out of other kinds of living."

Mary Kingsley's explorations of West Africa were remarkable, given that she spent the first 30 years of her life quietly at home. She was born in London on October 13, 1862. Her father, handsome and wealthy doctor George Kingsley, had married her mother, Mary Bailey—who had been his cook—just four days before. Though marriage saved Mary Bailey from being an outcast in the intensely moralistic environment of Victorian England, it could not make her fit into her husband's upper-middle-class world. For the rest of her life, she rarely ventured outside the Kingsleys' London home.

George Kingsley, meanwhile, wandered the globe, accompanying aristocratic employers to such faraway places as the Pacific islands of Fiji, Samoa, and Bora Bora—often for years at a time. His letters were full of enthralling tales of new experiences and near scrapes with death. But for the wife he left behind, life was monotonous and isolated. Although her daughter's birth was followed two years later by that of a son, Charles, motherhood had no great appeal for her. Like many unhappy Victorian women, she took refuge in illness that was at least partly imagined, spending the remainder of her life as a bedridden invalid.

Young Mary was responsible for taking care of the dark, closed-up house and her sick, demanding mother. As she later recalled, "The whole of my childhood and youth was spent at home, in the house and garden. The living world outside I saw little of, and cared less for, for I felt myself out of place. . . . I knew nothing of play or such things. But . . . I had a great amusing world of my own other people did not know or care about—that was the books in my father's library." Although Mary had no governess and was never sent to school, she somehow learned to read by the age of five. As a teenager, she was decidedly studious, enjoying science and tales of exploration. The books that most thrilled and inspired her were those written by explorers of Africa.

To Europeans, Africa was the "dark continent"—a mysterious land rich in gold and diamonds, home to exotic beasts and strange peoples, a place to freely pursue danger and untapped desires. European interest in Africa went back to classical times, but the nineteenth century marked the peak of exploration. Central to this exploration was trade, as Europeans sought ways to profit from their knowledge of Africa. The Portuguese, Belgians, French, Dutch, Germans, and British were all expanding their influence across the continent, competing to obtain territories with exclusive trading rights. This led to a scramble to carve Africa up into colonies that would be completely owned and governed by the European countries. Explorers played an integral part in colonization, scouting out trade routes, mapping the terrain, and making contact with the inhabitants. One of the most famous explorers was Richard Burton, whose 1876 book, *Two Trips to Gorilla Land*, was one of Mary's favorites. Burton explored extensively in the western portions of Africa that she later visited, and he encountered some of the same

Sir Richard Burton (1821-1890) won fame for his explorations of Asia and Africa and his translations of Eastern works such as The Arabian Nights.

indigenous tribes she would study. Unlike some other explorers of the time, Burton was more interested in studying the African people than in conquering them, a view that influenced Mary profoundly.

Mary's loneliness eased when her father returned home and relocated the family to Cambridge in 1884. Home to one of England's most prestigious universities, Cambridge was a thriving intellectual community. Mary found her first real female friends there, among the daughters and wives of professors and scholars. She also assisted her father with research and met many of his scientific friends. The pale, slim, shy young woman gained confidence as her horizons expanded, though she continued nursing her mother and running the household.

Then, very suddenly, Mary found her world turned upside down. When she knocked on her father's door one February morning in 1892, there was no answer. She turned the knob and walked in—only to discover that George Kingsley had died the night before in his sleep. Two months later, her mother also died. Only after her parents' deaths did Mary learn how narrowly she had escaped being born out of wedlock. She realized that her parents had not married out of love, and she could better understand her mother's unhappiness. Disturbed by this discovery and eager to escape the lonely house in cold, cloudy Cambridge, she decided to travel to the Canary Islands, a popular tourist destination off the northwest coast of Africa.

Mary booked a ticket as a passenger on an ocean liner and set sail in early June, arriving in the Canaries in late July. The beauty of the coastline, the endless blue of the sea, and the playfulness of the dolphins swimming alongside the ship inspired her. She spent weeks studying the local trade and industries and exploring the landscape on foot and by canoe. This first African experience was mostly a vacation, a chance to escape the confines of her life. By the time Mary returned to England in early autumn, however, she had made up her mind to journey to the west coast of Africa as soon as she was able. She wanted to see and learn—firsthand—as much about West Africa as she could.

By early August 1893, Mary Kingsley was ready to turn her dream into a reality. Her biggest obstacle was the duty of keeping house for her brother, Charley. Though the two had a strained relationship, she felt obligated to stay at home "as long as he wants me to do so." Luckily, Charley also liked to travel. As soon as he left on his own journey, she booked a ticket for West Africa, using her small inheritance to pay for the trip.

Kingsley wanted to experience Africa fully and needed to keep a tight budget once she arrived, so she planned to travel alone, eat local food, and take shelter in villages or sleep under the stars. This was a radical departure from the traveling style of most Europeans, who relied on armies of native servants to carry tents, beds, and canned food with them through the wilderness. Kingsley also decided to trade glass beads, fishhooks, tobacco, and other goods to the locals in exchange for rubber and ivory she could sell for a profit. Traveling as a trader would not only earn money, but it would also help her gain entrance to indigenous villages and start conversations with the inhabitants. Trade, she later wrote, "enables you to sit as an honored guest at far-away inland village fires [and do] things that being surrounded with an expedition of armed men must prevent your doing."

Kingsley took a nursing course, learning to treat injuries and common African diseases such as malaria and yellow fever. She packed her medical kit, heavy black skirts and white blouses, photography equipment, specimen bottles to hold the fish and insects she intended to gather, journals for her scientific observations and personal thoughts, a large knife, and a revolver. Before she left the country, Kingsley made out her will. She understood that she was undertaking a potentially dangerous journey from which she might not return.

Kingsley traveled to Africa with government officials and traders aboard a cargo ship called the *Lagos*. In late August, the *Lagos* reached the port of Freetown on the coast of Sierra Leone, a British colony founded as a home for freed slaves. Kingsley went ashore first thing in the morning and at last came face to face with the Africa she had come so far to find. It was market day, and throngs of people from different indigenous tribes—as well as former slaves from England, Canada, and the West Indies—

A Freetown market in 1910. On her visit, Kingsley saw people selling "kola nuts, old iron, antelope horns, monkey skins, porcupine quills, and snails."

crowded the streets. The bright colors and new sounds and smells amazed Kingsley. Later that day, she witnessed a rare sight: a swarm of locusts descending upon the town. (She often commented on the size and unpleasantness of African insects, noting that "75 per cent of West African insects sting, 5 per cent bite, and the rest are either permanently or temporarily parasitic on the human race.")

The *Lagos* set sail again that night, progressing farther down the coast to Portuguese Angola, where Kingsley's real journey into West Africa's interior began.

The ship reached its southernmost destination, the city of Saint Paul de Loanda, in September. From there, Kingsley took a smaller boat bound for Cabinda, a coastal enclave between the Congo Free State (now Democratic Republic of the Congo) and the Congo Français (now Republic of the Congo and Gabon). She spent several weeks at a trading post run by an Englishman, R. E. Dennett, who had been in the area for nearly 18 years. Dennett was an expert on the African religious belief known as fetishism, a subject that attracted Kingsley.

In studying fetishism, Kingsley noted that many tribes had witch doctors who guarded against magic and evil spirits. This picture shows a group of Sierra Leone women with a masked witch doctor in about 1900.

Canary
Islands

SIERRA
LEONE
Freetown

NIGERIA

CAMEROON

Calabar

Fernando Po

Libreville

CONGO
FRANÇAIS

CABINDA

CONGO FREE
STATE

St. Paul de Loanda

ANGOLA

ATLANTIC OCEAN

SOUTH
AFRICA
Simonstown

*This map of Africa shows the major places Mary
Kingsley visited on her journeys.*

Indigenous tribes saw spiritual power in the world around them—in the landscape and in objects (fetishes) such as shells and carved wood. One of the central points of fetishism was the idea that all diseases were caused by magic and evil spirits; illnesses always had a spiritual cause, rather than a natural source such as bacteria. Understanding fetishism became the major goal of Kingsley's travels.

Kingsley visited the Congo Free State and then went by land to the Congo Français, where she spent at least two months. She pressed deeper into the country's interior, often alone. Walking through the thick, dark forest frightened Kingsley at first, but she soon came to appreciate the landscape. "Day by day," she wrote, "as you get trained to your surroundings, you see more and more, and a whole world grows up gradually out of the gloom before your eyes. Snakes, beetles, bats, and beasts people the region that at first seemed lifeless." Soon, Kingsley could identify all the various grasses, vines, and trees of the forests, and she learned the best way to catch fish. She encountered a number of local tribes, some of whom had never seen a European before, but most of whom received her with hospitality. She felt she was beginning to truly understand Africa.

After traveling north by ship to Cameroon and Nigeria, Kingsley set sail for England in early December. By the time she disembarked in gray, rainy Liverpool in January, she no longer recognized England as her home. Instead, coming back to the London house she shared with Charley felt like a kind of exile. All she could think about was returning to West Africa. Kingsley spent long hours in her study, surrounded by African artifacts, with the heat turned up to a tropical temperature. She studied anthropology (the science of the development and social behaviors of human cultures) with the goal of writing an analysis of African law and religion. Kingsley also continued her work in biology. She met with Albert Charles Günther, keeper of the zoological department at the British Museum and author of *Introduction to the Study of*

Albert Charles Günther (1830-1914), a friend of Mary Kingsley's uncle Charles, became her major scientific mentor.

Fishes, which she had used as a handbook for studying fish in Africa. She showed him the collection of fish she had brought back in large bottles of alcohol. Though astonished by the amateurish way in which she had preserved her specimens, Günther was impressed by Kingsley's work. When she told him she intended to return to West Africa, he gave her better equipment and commissioned her to collect freshwater fish from the little-known region between the Niger and Congo Rivers.

As soon as Charley left on another trip, Mary Kingsley was off to West Africa again, pursuing her dual interests of "fish and fetish." Just before Christmas 1894, she boarded the steamer *Batanga* and set sail for the third time. Traveling south down the West African coast, Kingsley made her first major stop at the island of Fernando Po (now Bioko, part of Equatorial Guinea) to study its indigenous inhabitants, a people called the Bubi. She spent several weeks visiting Bubi villages scattered around the island, and through careful observation she was able to discern much about the tribe's traditions, economy, religion, and initiation rites. Ultimately, Kingsley devoted more than 20 pages of her first book to a discussion of the Bubi, and her writing is a model study of a little-known society.

Kingsley boarded the *Batanga* again and sailed back north to Calabar, Nigeria, arriving in early February. For the next two months she made short trips out from Calabar, canoeing up and down the Cross River and hiking through the nearby forest. She collected fish and insects, as well as information about the various peoples who lived in the area—the Igbo, the Ibibio, and the Effik. On one occasion, an eight-foot-long crocodile nearly climbed into her canoe. Though it must have been a terrifying experience, Kingsley later described it with humor: "[The crocodile] chose to get his front paws over the stern of my canoe, and endeavored to improve our acquaintance. I had to retire to the bows, to keep the balance . . . and fetch him a clip on the snout with a paddle, when he withdrew."

In May, Kingsley traveled farther down the coast to the port of Glass, a short distance from Libreville, the capital of Congo Français. From there, she set off up the Ogooué River, first on a paddle steamer and then on her own, in search of fish and indigenous tribes. To do so, she had to learn to steer a dugout canoe—no easy task, for the river's current was fast and strong. She later declared, "There are only two things I am proud of—one is that Dr. Günther has approved of my fishes, and the other is that I can paddle an Ogooué canoe. Pace, style, steering and all . . . as if I were an Ogooué African."

In late July, Kingsley returned downriver to the settlement of Kangwe. From there, she set off on one of her most ambitious journeys yet: an overland expedition across the uncharted territory between the Ogooué and Remboué Rivers. This area was inhabited by the Fang people, a tribe known for their strength as warriors and

Kingsley (center, to left of flag) on the Ogooué River, which she thought to be "as full of life and beauty and passion as any symphony Beethoven ever wrote."

their skill as craftsmen. Among Europeans, the Fang had a reputation for savagery and were even thought to be cannibals. Kingsley, however, was more interested in the tribe's strong resistance to missionaries. The fact that Fang culture had remained largely intact made it ideal for her studies, and she was willing to endure great hardships to reach Fang villages that had not yet been altered by European influence. Accompanied by several Africans, she began the difficult journey along the rivers northwest of Kangwe. Kingsley and her companions then left the rivers and made their way on foot through dense rain forests, trekking as many as 25 miles a day. The closer they got to the Remboué River, the more hazardous the journey became. The group braved a series of treacherous tidal swamps before reaching the Remboué a week later.

Along the way, Kingsley traveled from village to village, observing the Fang people's way of life. She was especially interested in their crafts, which included basket making, pottery, netting, weaving, and ironwork. Her anthropological study of the Fang eventually became an entire chapter of her first book. Kingsley felt a close kinship with the Fang, writing, "these Africans have more of

This photograph of a group of Fang warriors was probably taken by Mary Kingsley herself.

the qualities I like than any other tribe I have met. . . . The Fang is full of fire, temper, intelligence, and go." Yet she never came to understand their spiritual beliefs and always hoped to be able to return to their villages one day.

Kingsley spent several more months in West Africa, and in September she became the first European woman to climb Mount Cameroon. By the end of November, however, she was back in England. As she disembarked from the ship, she found a reporter waiting for her at the dock. Kingsley did not know it yet, but with this third journey she had become a celebrity. The public was fascinated by her African travels. Urged to give her opinions about Africa to the press, she did so cautiously and truthfully. She fought the common misperception that Africa was inhabited by barbarous cultures that needed to be civilized by Europeans. Kingsley stressed that Africans possessed a strong sense of honor and justice, and they had highly developed laws and religion. Although she did not question Europe's perceived right to govern Africa, she argued that colonial powers should rule indirectly, using existing African government instead of imposing their own. Kingsley wanted to preserve indigenous societies in Africa, and she feared that Europeans would exploit the resources and destroy local culture. "What we do in Africa today, a thousand years hence there will be Africans to thrive or suffer for it," she warned.

Though Kingsley's political views were controversial for the time, her scientific expertise was undeniable.

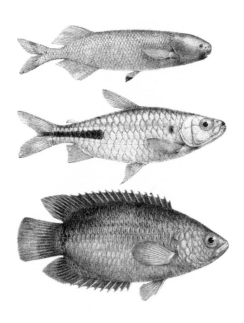

Three fish species discovered by and named for Mary Kingsley (top to bottom): Mormyrus kingsleyae, Alestes kingsleyae, *and* Ctenopoma kingsleyae

Many of the 65 species of fish and 18 species of reptiles among her specimens proved to be valuable discoveries, and eventually three entirely new species of fish were named after her. When Kingsley gave public lectures about her travels, accompanied by slides, her audiences numbered as many as 1,700 people at a time. Her dynamic lecturing built up public anticipation for her first book. A combination of anthropological observations of African tribes, scientific information about plants and animals, and stories of Kingsley's own adventures—all written in a spirited, conversational style—*Travels in West Africa* was published in January 1897 and became an instant best-seller. Kingsley published another well-received volume,

West African Studies, in 1899. Her increasing celebrity brought her a busy social life, though she concentrated on earning money for another trip to West Africa.

In 1899, war broke out in South Africa between Great Britain and Dutch settlers, or "Boers," over territory and gold mines. Kingsley promptly applied to the government as an army nurse, hoping that if she were sent to South Africa she could also report on the war for newspapers, collect specimens of fish, and eventually return to West Africa. On March 10, 1900, Kingsley boarded the *Moor*, a ship carrying troops and artillery to the Boer War. Three weeks later, she arrived in Simonstown, near the Cape of Good Hope on South Africa's southwest coast. She took up medical duty at a makeshift hospital, where one doctor and two other nurses cared for more than 200 sick and wounded Boer prisoners of war. The hospital was inevitably an infectious place, and in May, Kingsley fell ill with typhoid fever. Though the doctor assured her that she would recover, she knew better. Her one request was to be buried at sea.

Mary Kingsley died on June 3, 1900, at the age of 37. The doctor honored her last wish, and she was buried off the Cape of Good Hope with full military honors. After her death, the Mary Kingsley Society of West Africa (later renamed the African Society and still in existence today) was established to study native customs and beliefs. Kingsley, who felt more alive in Africa than anyplace else, would certainly have been pleased with this memorial.

LIBRARY
DEXTER SCHOOLS
DEXTER, NM 88230

*"Adventure is my only reason for living," said
Alexandra David-Neel (1868-1969). At the age of
87, she posed for this picture in Tibetan dress,
surrounded by some of the artifacts she collected
during her many adventures in Asia.*

2

Alexandra David-Neel
Pilgrim in Tibet

*O*n the way to the forbidden city of Lhasa, Tibet, in 1923, two travelers came to a fork in the road. Both the 55-year-old Frenchwoman Alexandra David-Neel and her young companion—Yongden, a Buddhist monk—knew that whichever path they chose, they would face danger. The first road passed villages and monasteries, so finding food would not be difficult. By coming into contact with so many people, however, David-Neel would risk discovery, for Tibet was off-limits to Europeans. Disguised as an old Tibetan woman, David-Neel was determined to become the first European woman to enter Lhasa. If officials learned of her presence, she would be sent back across the border into China. Given all the hardships she and Yongden had braved to come this far, the idea of abandoning her journey was impossible to bear.

The second road was a mountain track through the wilderness. On this route, they would have to scale two very high passes and cross a large tract of land in between. Snow and rough terrain would make it hazardous. Yet chances were very good that they would not meet a single soul. Isolation lessened the risk of discovery, but it also meant that they would have to find their own food. In addition, they might encounter robbers who would steal their few possessions and perhaps even kill them.

For a few moments, the two travelers hesitated at the crossroads. While Yongden waited for her decision, David-Neel stood contemplating the danger and the strenuousness of the mountain road. But she also considered its beauty, and the fact that very few pilgrims to Lhasa chose to travel this way. Alexandra David-Neel always preferred to do what others did not. "Let us take the mountain road," she told Yongden at last.

Alexandra David was born in Paris on October 24, 1868. She was the only child of Alexandrine Borghmans, a Belgian, and Louis Pierre David, a Frenchman. Louis was a journalist and political activist who was a friend of Victor Hugo, one of France's most famous writers. Alexandra adored her father, but he was old by the time she was born, and in some ways he remained aloof to the needs of a small child. Alexandra felt rejected by her mother, who she saw as a cold, neglectful woman. From an early age, Alexandra was aware of the unhappiness of her parents' marriage. Though her childhood was materially comfortable, with governesses, English and music lessons, and fine clothes, it was also full of emotional tension.

Like many lonely children, Alexandra sought an escape in books, such as Jules Verne's fantasy stories and James Fenimore Cooper's adventure novels about life in the rugged young country of America. She dreamed of travel, later recalling, "I could remain for hours near a railway line, fascinated by the glittering rails and fancying the many lands toward which they led. But . . . my imagination did not evoke towns, buildings, gay crowds, or stately pageants; I dreamed of wild hills, immense deserted steppes and impassable landscapes of glaciers!" Seeking freedom and solitude, Alexandra ran away from home and boarding school repeatedly, beginning when she was just five years old. "I craved to go beyond the garden gate, to follow the road that passed it by, and to set out for the unknown," she wrote.

As she grew older, Alexandra pored over books about China, Japan, and India. She spent many afternoons in the Musée Guimet, a museum devoted to the antiquities of the Far East. It had a magnificent library in which she could read about religion, geography, history, and folklore. By her early twenties, Alexandra was busy learning Sanskrit, an ancient language of India used in literary and religious writings. She was also deeply involved in theosophy, a mystical religious philosophy that had elements of Buddhism. (Based on the teachings of the Buddha, an ancient Indian mystic, Buddhism is an Asian religion that seeks enlightenment—a total release from earthly desires and suffering—through good conduct, wisdom, and meditation.) In 1891, when Alexandra was 23, she received a small inheritance from her godmother. The money enabled her to spend more than a year in India and Ceylon (now Sri Lanka). Gripped by poverty and famine, the places she had dreamed of for so long were different than she had expected, but she found the harsh reality no less fascinating. Once she returned to France, her desire to travel farther into the East only grew stronger.

Unfortunately, traveling required money—which Alexandra did not have. Her father had lost his wealth in the stock market. Although few professions were open to women, she knew that she could find a paying career in music, for she had shown promise as a pianist, singer, and composer. Alexandra joined the Opéra-Comique as a soprano. Touring with this and other companies, she visited Greece, Indochina, and the North African country of Tunisia. It was there that Alexandra met her distant cousin Philippe-François Neel, an engineer. The two were married in August 1904.

Alexandra quickly discovered that the mutual responsibilities of marriage were not for her. The couple

Philippe Neel not only supported his wife financially during her travels, but he also stored her belongings, shipped goods for her, and arranged to publish her manuscripts.

parted ways; she traveled throughout Europe, writing and studying, while he remained in North Africa. Though Philippe financially supported Alexandra's travels and remained her chief correspondent and closest European friend, the two never lived together for any real length of time during the nearly 40 years of their marriage.

In August 1911, Alexandra David-Neel set sail for India, leaving Europe on her own terms at last. Although she did not realize it at the time, she would stay in Asia for the next 14 years. As soon as she arrived, David-Neel dove into study of Sanskrit and Indian philosophy, traveling throughout the country to meet with philosophers and teachers. The recognition she received from them pleased her. "You cannot imagine the glamour and prestige a European Buddhist enjoys in Asia," she wrote to her husband. She soon realized, however, that there could be more to her experience in Asia than glamour and prestige.

In early 1912, David-Neel decided that an interview with the Dalai Lama, the spiritual and political head of Tibetan Buddhists, would make an interesting article for a French magazine. (The Dalai Lama had fled to India when the Chinese army invaded Tibet in February 1910; he returned to Tibet when the troops retreated later in 1912.) To her amazement and honor, he agreed to meet with her—the first private audience ever granted a European woman. When she was ushered into his presence, David-Neel told the Dalai Lama, "The religious doctrines of Tibet are not understood in Europe. I am hoping you will enlighten me." Impressed by her curiosity and her knowledge of Buddhism, the Dalai Lama spoke to her for nearly an hour, stressing the value of a life of poverty, simplicity, and contemplation, and the unique freedoms such a life enabled. They spoke in English, and before they parted, the Dalai Lama's final words to her were "Learn the Tibetan language!"

In the autumn of the following year, David-Neel did exactly that. She had become a close friend of Sidkeong Tulku, the crown prince of Sikkim (a small area on Tibet's southern border). Educated at Oxford University in England, he was also a lama—a Tibetan Buddhist monk—and together he and David-Neel visited

Sidkeong Tulku (fourth from right) took David-Neel (third from left) on her first trip into Tibet in 1912.

villages and monasteries, climbed into the foothills of the Himalayan Mountains, and discussed Buddhism for hours. The prince offered her the use of an apartment in the Buddhist monastery of Podang outside the Sikkim capital of Gangtok, where she found a teacher to help her learn Tibetan. David-Neel also asked one of the monks if he could find a young boy to assist her on her travels. The boy chosen for this role was a 15-year-old named Yongden, who—like David-Neel—longed to see the world. David-Neel and Yongden would travel and study together until his death some 40 years later.

Yongden served as a companion who could share David-Neel's experiences and ideas. He would also be a witness to her great accomplishments and a caregiver in her old age.

In August 1914, World War I broke out in Europe, making a return to France even less appealing for David-Neel. Instead, she decided to cross a few miles into Tibet from Sikkim in order to visit a monastery called Chorten Nyima. In this small religious and scholarly community in a remote, rocky region, she encountered four Buddhist nuns. Despite being snowed in for half the year, threatened by starvation and wild animals, they had chosen to spend their lives in solitude and study. The women told David-Neel that there were small communities of nuns scattered throughout the mountains, and there were even women who lived as hermits in caves or traveled alone as pilgrims. This was a way of life David-Neel had never known to be available to women. Now that she had seen for herself that it was possible, her own longing for a life of spiritual adventure intensified.

The nuns told David-Neel about a hermit lama who lived in a cave in Sikkim at an elevation of 13,000 feet. Intrigued, David-Neel went to visit him and convinced him to take her on as a sort of apprentice. With the lama's blessing, she spent the winter of 1914-1915 in a nearby cave of her own, with Yongden and some servants in an adjacent hut. Although the weather was fierce and

David-Neel sits in front of her hermitage high in the mountains of northern Sikkim.

living conditions were rough, this quiet life of study and long walks, without any definite schedule or pressures, appealed to David-Neel enormously. "I feel that the hermit's life, free of what we call 'the goods and pleasures of the world,' is the most wonderful life of all," she wrote to her husband.

In the spring, David-Neel and Yongden again crossed into Tibet, this time to visit the Panchen Lama (equal to the Dalai Lama in spiritual rank, but with less political power) at the Tashilhunpo monastery in Shigatze. When they returned to India, David-Neel learned that the British government of India was demanding she leave the country because she had crossed into Tibet without a pass. Hoping to expand its empire into Tibet, Britain had restricted the entrance of foreigners into the country, reinforcing Tibet's traditional isolation. One of the least accessible countries on Earth due to its high altitude and rough terrain, Tibet had remained a mystery to the rest of the world for thousands of years. It had closed itself to outsiders, resisting most foreign influence until the British to the west, the Russians to the north, and the Chinese to the north and east had begun competing for control of the area in the early twentieth century.

To David-Neel, these governments' attempts to keep others out of Tibet were ridiculous: "What right had they to erect barriers around a country which was not even lawfully theirs?" She believed that false political boundaries should not interfere with an individual's right to travel where he or she chose, and the British government's orders provoked her rebellious streak. "What decided me to go to Lhasa," she later wrote, "was above all, the absurd prohibition which closes Tibet." She chose to risk fine and imprisonment to return to Tibet as soon as possible.

Now that she was officially banned from India, the only way into Tibet lay through China. Accompanied by Yongden, David-Neel journeyed to China via Burma (now Myanmar), Japan, and Korea. They traveled at a leisurely pace, staying at Buddhist monasteries along the way, and arrived in China's capital, Peking (now Beijing), in October 1917. In late January, they set out again.

The cart that carried David-Neel during her journey from Peking in 1918

China was ravaged by plague and civil wars, so they traveled in the safety of a wealthy Tibetan lama's large caravan. Seven months and 1,600 miles later, after braving illness and gunfire along the way, they reached north-central China. There, they stopped at Kumbum, a Buddhist monastery that dated back to the sixteenth century.

Though the monastery did not traditionally admit women, the monks made an exception in David-Neel's case. She was old, she was learned, and she had the blessings of the Dalai Lama and the Panchen Lama—all things the monks valued enormously. Here, David-Neel resumed her quiet life of study and contemplation. Rising early, she spent her days reading rare texts from the monastery's library and translating them into English and French. In addition, she meditated and listened to sacred music with the monks.

David-Neel stayed contentedly at the monastery for nearly three years before she and Yongden set forth into the world once again. Their goal was Tibet—specifically the holy city of Lhasa, the spiritual heart of Tibetan Buddhism. For centuries, European adventurers had struggled to penetrate this fascinating, forbidden city; a few had succeeded, but many others had been turned back by soldiers and officials, the formidable mountains, or the harsh winter. David-Neel had studied these travelers' tales, and she learned from their mistakes. She would travel modestly, with only a few servants and no valuables, so as not to attract attention. Since she could speak Tibetan and knew local culture and customs, she could conceal her European identity if necessary. And to avoid suspicion, she would take a flexible, roundabout route to the border. In fact, it took David-Neel three years to reach Tibet.

Given her nomadic existence during this time, where David-Neel was and when is hard to establish. She was happy to wander wherever she chose, and time was of little importance to her. The fact that much of the country she traveled over was not accurately mapped makes it even more difficult to trace her path. Essentially, she and Yongden made a series of loops through China. First they traveled south to the Sichuan province, where they attempted to cross into Tibet but were turned back by Chinese soldiers. Next, they traveled north to the Gobi Desert and Mongolia before circling south again, through Sichuan to the farthest southwest corner of China—the province of Yunnan, where they prepared to cross the border into Tibet.

The vast country of China was difficult for the government to regulate, and travelers, especially in the sparsely populated western regions, faced constant danger from bandits. Several other French explorers were robbed or killed or had simply disappeared in the area through which David-Neel traveled. At more than 50 years old and barely five feet tall, she may have seemed defenseless—yet she was never attacked. She carried a pistol, but she never fired a shot.

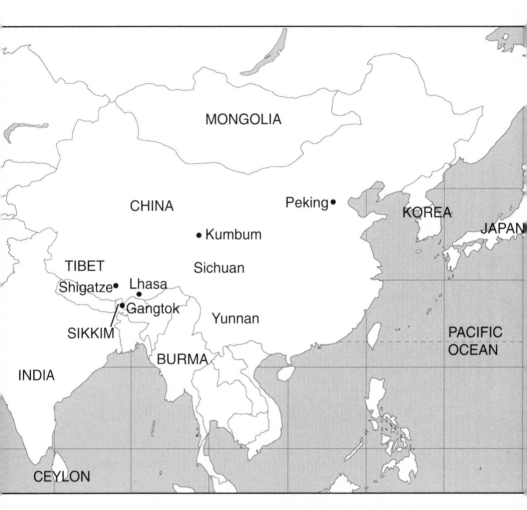

Although David-Neel's path to Lhasa is difficult to trace, this map shows some of the places she visited along the way.

Only once did David-Neel make a scene and threaten violence, and that was when soldiers met up with her not far from the Tibetan border. The soldiers ordered her back, but David-Neel cried, "Give me my revolver! I will kill myself rather than turn back! Then," she added craftily, "the authorities will find my body and believe that you have murdered me, and you will be forced to suffer for the crime!" Completely taken by surprise and unwilling to have anything more to do with this strange Frenchwoman, the soldiers told her to "Go away quietly, please."

In October 1923, near the Kha Karpo mountain range that separated Yunnan from Tibet, David-Neel dismissed her servants and slipped away on foot with Yongden. She carried little more than a tent, an aluminum pot, a bowl, a spoon, a knife, a pair of chopsticks, her money belt, her gun, and a walking stick with an iron spike that she could use to defend herself. She disguised herself as a Tibetan peasant woman, darkening her hair and skin and dressing in rags. Then she and Yongden began the final stage of their journey, crossing into Tibet by the Dokar Pass (elevation 14,890 feet). They trekked through a mountainous, snowy wilderness, climbing summits of up to 19,000 feet. Often, they hiked for 19 hours straight and went without food or water for more than 30 hours. They successfully evaded British, Tibetan, and Chinese authorities by traveling through lonely and difficult terrain, often at night. They slept outdoors or in huts and begged for their food, eating whatever was given

One of David-Neel's camps in the mountains.
Inspired by the scenery, she wrote, "every moment of
this free wandering life is an enchantment."

them. Despite these hardships, David-Neel loved the
landscape, calling it "grand beyond all description."

For the last 400 miles of their journey, David-Neel
and Yongden left the more remote paths and joined the
China Road, the great caravan trail to Lhasa. Here,
David-Neel found herself surrounded by people. She
knew that her disguise was not necessarily protection
against being found out; a gesture, a mispronounced
word, some small slip could give her away. Then there
was the toll bridge where they would have to pay a fee and

obtain a pass. For weeks, David-Neel dreaded reaching the bridge, where she was afraid her European identity would be discovered. When the time came, Yongden went inside the checkpoint while David-Neel waited outside and prayed. But no one paid any attention to her at all. Having come this far, she knew that she would reach Lhasa at last.

In February 1924, David-Neel and Yongden arrived in Lhasa. Thousands of pilgrims had descended upon the city for the month-long New Year's celebrations, and David-Neel was able to move about without detection, visiting as many places as she possibly could. She watched religious ceremonies and processions, went to tea houses and the main bazaar, and bought books to bring back to Europe. She even mustered the courage to tour the Potala, the magnificent fortress palace of the Dalai Lama. After about two months in Lhasa, she and Yongden left the city on horseback, headed for India. She wanted to confront the British officials there and show them that she had made it to Lhasa. At the border town of Gyantze, David Macdonald, the British trade agent, greeted David-Neel with a mixture of astonishment and admiration. He wrote in his files that she not only spoke admirable English, but she also knew "Tibetan like a native." He noted that with "immense courage and vitality" she had "undergone incredible hardships." From him, David-Neel received written proof that she had been to Lhasa.

David-Neel (center), in her Tibetan disguise, sits
with Yongden (left) and an unidentified girl in front
of the Potala in Lhasa.

David-Neel returned to Paris in the summer of
1925, accompanied by Yongden, who lived with her as an
adopted son until his death. For the next four decades,
she enjoyed prestige throughout Europe. Her rare firsthand experiences made her the reigning expert on Tibet
and Buddhism. She published numerous books on her
travels and gave lectures at universities. Yet in spite of the

respect she commanded, David-Neel was no longer happy in Paris, finding city life stifling. In 1927, she bought a house in the countryside in the south of France—near the Alps, which reminded her of Tibet. She named the house Samten Dzong, meaning "Fortress of Meditation." There, she studied, wrote, and lived the life she had followed in Asia. Age did not rob her of her energy: at age 68, she returned to Tibet via Germany, Russia, and China, staying for eight years (until the invasion of China by Japan forced her to flee).

Shortly before her death in 1969 at the age of 100, she set down in writing what she believed to be the secret of her success: "Some will think that I have been uncommonly lucky. I shall not disagree; but luck has a cause, like anything else, and I believe there exists a mental attitude capable of shaping circumstances more or less according to one's wishes." Alexandra David-Neel was clearly a woman who shaped her life according to the needs of her independent and adventurous spirit.

"The air and sunlight, the adventure and romance of exploration are full compensation to some of us for discomfort, hardship, and danger," said Harriet Chalmers Adams (1875-1937), who experienced both romance and danger on her journeys through Latin America and around the world.

3

Harriet Chalmers Adams
In the Footsteps of the
Conquistadors

*D*eep in the jungle east of the Andes Mountains, Harriet Chalmers Adams was awakened in the middle of the night by the noise of beating wings. As she later liked to tell the tale, the eerie sound reminded her of the purring of a hundred cats. She could not see anything distinctly in the intense darkness. She could not even muster the will to rise, as if she had been hypnotized by the sound. Eventually, she drew her thick veil over her face and fell back asleep.

In the morning, Harriet discovered the ominous source of the night's activity. All of her companions had bloody wounds in their throats, chests, and necks. When Harriet asked what had happened, one of the men told her that they had been attacked by vampire bats. The bats infested the forest, and the explorers had unknowingly rested in the thick of them. When the bats attacked, the purring sound supposedly hypnotized the men. Then the bats descended upon their necks, punctured them with their sharp teeth, and fed on their blood. The pack animals, too, had been attacked, and one of the mules lay dead. Harriet alone had escaped without injury, because of the veil she wore.

It was April 1904, and Harriet Chalmers Adams and her husband, Frank, had trekked across the Andes Mountains of Peru to a region known as "the inside"—a largely unexplored jungle that stretched some 3,000 miles to the Atlantic Ocean. They traveled on horseback, often for 12-to-14-hour stretches at a time, carrying only the bare necessities: blankets, food, medicine, rifles, and cameras. They faced rainstorms, blizzards, avalanches, and treacherous paths. On one occasion, Harriet's horse tripped over a rock and threw her headfirst into a stream. "I've been in tight places, have seen harrowing things," Harriet later declared. Yet despite the hardships she endured, she never regretted any of her experiences. "I've . . . never faced a difficulty which a woman, as well as a man, could not surmount; never felt a fear of danger, never lacked courage to protect myself," she said. After all, the challenges she weathered led her to exhilarating places. In the same forest haunted by the vampire bats, one especially steep, slippery path brought her face to face with the most beautiful canyon she had ever seen, full of ferns, pink and white begonias, orchids, waterfalls, and vivid butterflies.

With her self-confidence and her love for the places she visited, Harriet Chalmers Adams became an authority on Latin America (the region south of the United States, mostly made up of Spanish- and Portuguese-speaking countries). She also became one of the most famous and widely traveled American explorers of her time.

Harriet inherited her love of adventure from her Scots-Canadian father, Alexander Chalmers. As a young man, he had come to California seeking his fortune in the gold mines along the American River. In 1868, he gave up mining for retailing, opening Chalmers Brothers Dry Goods and Carpets with his brother George in Stockton, California. Here, in the lovely San Joaquin Valley just east of San Francisco, Alexander married Frances Wilkins and settled down. Harriet, their first child, was born on October 22, 1875.

Alexander never lost his restlessness, and he frequently took Harriet with him on his travels. "My father had no boys, so I took a boy's place," she later explained. "I was an explorer when I was too young to realize it." At the age of eight, she joined her father on a horseback trip through the San Joaquin and Sacramento Valleys and up the California coast. When she was 14, the two spent an entire year exploring California on horseback. Such journeys with her father, Harriet recalled, made her into "one who wished to go to the ends of the earth . . . to see and study the people of all lands."

Because Harriet and her younger sister, Anna, were educated at home by their parents and tutors, missing school was never an issue. It was Alexander Chalmers who taught his eldest daughter much of what she most valued: how to research the places she visited and how to hold on to her impressions of them by recording her adventures in writing. Harriet had a natural affinity for languages and could quickly pick up the speech of a particular place, ultimately learning Spanish, Portuguese, Italian, German, and French.

Harriet eventually found someone else in Stockton who shared her adventurous spirit. On October 5, 1899, when she was almost 24, she married 31-year-old electrical engineer Frank Adams. During the first year of their marriage they traveled through California by horse, train, and the newly invented automobile. To finance longer journeys, Frank sought out jobs that would take him and Harriet to exotic regions. In 1900, the couple traveled to Mexico. While Frank worked on an engineering survey, Harriet became enthralled with the archaeological sites where explorers were unearthing evidence of ancient indigenous civilizations.

*Frank
Adams*

In 1904, Frank was offered a job inspecting Central and South American mines. Thrilled at the chance to explore more of Latin America, Harriet read 15 books about the region in preparation for their trip. Once Frank had finished his inspections, they planned to retrace the trail of the Spanish conquistadors who had explored and colonized Latin America in the sixteenth century. Harriet wanted to study the Incas—one of the indigenous groups who had then lived in South America—and their civilization's transformation by the Spaniards. She would carefully record what she observed on the journey, with the goal of later lecturing and writing about her experiences. Frank had taught her photography, and she hoped to document their travels in both photographs and motion pictures.

This map of South America shows the countries and some of the major cities that the Adamses visited during their trip.

The Adamses set sail on January 9, 1904, traveling down the west coast of Mexico and into Central America. After stops in Guatemala, El Salvador, Panama, and Ecuador, they arrived in Callao, Peru, on March 2. From there, they made their way inland to the large capital city, Lima, which was rocked by an earthquake during their stay. Returning to Callao on March 26, they boarded a ship to the port of Mollendo, in southern Peru. From there, they traveled northeast to Arequipa to acclimatize themselves to the high altitudes they would experience during their journey to the eastern slopes of the Andes Mountains, where Frank would inspect mines belonging to the Inca Mining and Rubber Company.

On the 1,000-mile trek across the Andes, Frank and Harriet traveled on horseback with a guide. They slept in the open or on the floors of huts, eating native food. Pack animals carried their essentials, including the heavy photography equipment. As they climbed higher into the mountains, eventually reaching the Pass of Aricoma at an elevation of 17,000 feet, the animals as well as the humans suffered from altitude sickness. Harriet used smelling salts (a combination of chemicals and perfume, used by ladies of the time to relieve faintness and headaches) to revive not only herself, but also her mule. Given that the paths they traveled could be extremely nar-row—one was only 30 inches wide and hugged a cliff with a straight drop into the canyon 1,000 feet below—clear-headed steadiness was essential to survival.

After reaching the mines, the Adamses ventured into the unexplored jungle region known as "the inside," then climbed back into the Andes. Like many people and animals before them, they made their way onto the Old Inca Highway, an ancient road that predated the Spanish conquest. Traveling by mule cart, they reached Cuzco, a city in Peru that had once been the capital of the Inca empire. There, Harriet became interested in the Quechua Indians (descendants of the ancient Incas who lived throughout the Andes), and she documented their speech, customs, and way of life in photographs and writing. From Cuzco, Harriet and Frank headed north to the majestic ruins of Ollantaytambo, built with rocks that had been transported across the mountains from distant quarries. The Adamses also visited the Valley of Yucay, an area seldom seen by outsiders. "Those were long days in the saddle, with little food and less water," Harriet later wrote. "At night we slept on the ground, wrapped in our blankets, at times finding shelter in a ruined temple. . . . We met no travelers save the highland Indians, and picked up a few words of their tongue. I felt that we had left civilization far behind. Even the Spanish colonial days faded. We were in the old Peru."

By July, they were heading back towards the coast. In Arequipa, Harriet and Frank climbed Mount Misti, a 19,200-foot peak. The couple then boarded a ship to Chile, where they spent more than a month before continuing on through the Strait of Magellan at the southernmost

One of the last places constructed by the Inca before the Spanish conquest, Ollantaytambo was never finished. A modern town was built on its foundations, but Incan ruins still stand on the mountainside above.

tip of South America. They then rode the length of Argentina on horseback, traveled by river to Bolivia, rode through Paraguay and Uruguay, went north by ship along the coast of Brazil to Rio de Janeiro, traveled along the Amazon River, and spent three months exploring the rain forest. Finally, they headed north to French Guiana, Colombia, and Panama.

By the time Harriet and Frank returned to the United States in May 1906, they had covered more than 40,000 miles, crossing the Andes Mountains four times. Harriet had kept a journal of their travels, written 50 detailed letters to her family, and taken 3,000 photographs and dozens of motion-picture films. Seeking to share her newfound and hard-won knowledge, she wrote to Gilbert Grosvenor, president of the National Geographic Society, outlining her travel in Latin America and asking if she might give a speech. Grosvenor was so intrigued by this amazing summary that he invited Harriet to Washington, D.C., to lecture to the society. This meeting grew into a lifelong friendship with Grosvenor and a long-standing relationship with the National Geographic Society. She would write a total of 22 articles for *National Geographic* magazine, often illustrated with her own photographs.

The Washington lecture was enthusiastically received, and soon Harriet Chalmers Adams began traveling across the country speaking to businesses, towns, clubs, and colleges. Lecturing became a crucial part of her career. It allowed her an outlet for speaking about all that she had seen and experienced, and it also helped to educate the public about a part of the world she believed most Americans knew "comparatively little about." Furthermore, Adams's speaking engagements provided her with funds for future travel. She initially earned about $40 per lecture, but she later commanded as much as $600 for a single appearance. Adams also began publishing articles in magazines. It was only a matter of time before publishers invited her to write books about her experiences, and in 1910, she signed a contract with Doubleday Page and Company.

HARRIET CHALMERS ADAMS

The South American Traveler, will give

An Illustrated Lecture on "Peru"

AT THE Y. M. C. A. HALL

Tuesday Evening, February 26, 1907

MRS. ADAMS has recently returned from a three years' journey through South America, during which time she visited every country on the continent and many places never before seen by a white woman. In her lecture on the Land of the Incas, Mrs. Adams tells of her wonderful trip of more than a thousand miles in the saddle, when, after crossing the eastern chain of the Andes at a height of more than 17,000 feet, she reached the vast forest land of the head waters of the Amazon.

Two Hundred Color Pictures Illustrate the Story

THE PROCEEDS OF THIS LECTURE WILL BE USED FOR THE FURNISHING OF THE Y. M. C. A. GAME ROOM

Reserved Seats   -   -   Fifty Cents

Tickets on Sale at Hodge's Drug Store, February 19th

AN AYMARA, A TYPE OF UPPER PERU

This advertisement for one of Adams's lectures about her travels features her photograph of an Aymara Indian from Peru.

That same year, the Adamses traveled to Cuba, Haiti, and the Dominican Republic, tracing the path of Christopher Columbus's voyages. Since she had already seen so much of Latin America, Harriet decided to visit every country in the world that had ever been possessed by Spain or Portugal—about 20 nations in all. She traveled, often alone (Frank was busy with his own work), to Europe, West and North Africa, and many islands in the Pacific and Atlantic Oceans.

In addition to studying Spanish heritage, Harriet Chalmers Adams was fascinated by North and South America's indigenous tribes. In the spring of 1913, she traveled to the Far East to do research into her theory that

*During her Asian tour, Harriet Chalmers Adams
posed with a camel in the Gobi Desert, which spans
Mongolia and part of China.*

the Native American peoples had Asian roots. Adams
speculated that the Inca, Quechua, Maya, Toltec, Aztec,
and Pueblo Indians were all descendants of Asian peoples
who had come to America by sea long ago, paddling large
canoes similar to those used by modern South Sea
islanders. She based her conclusions on the physical like-
nesses of the Native American and Asian peoples as well as
on similarities in their customs and languages. Adams
believed that a study of the Malay, Chinese, and Tibetan
people would illuminate the history of the early Americans.
In the course of her research, she traveled to Hawaii, the

Philippines (where she spent nearly three months living among headhunting tribes), Japan, Borneo, Malaysia, Singapore, and China.

In June 1916, Adams embarked on a very different kind of journey. World War I had broken out in Europe, and she set sail for France as a war correspondent for *Harper's Magazine*. While she was there, she also studied war conditions on behalf of the American Fund for French Wounded, gaining access to trenches at the front

When Adams visited the front lines, a young French soldier picked her a bouquet of flowers. Reporters gathered around to capture the moment, and this image appeared throughout the world press.

as well as to hospitals and prisons. She was the only woman allowed to visit the front lines and to photograph French battle scenes. Enduring bombing and gunfire vividly drove home to Adams the brutal realities of the war. Once she returned to the United States (which had not yet entered the war) the following October, she began to travel around the country speaking about the French war effort. Sometimes lecturing as many as six times in one day, she raised thousands of dollars for war relief.

While traveling from lecture to lecture, Adams visited every Native American reservation and historic site she could. In particular, she studied Native American languages, looking for similarities between them that would support her belief that the different indigenous groups had one central origin. Having found affinities between the languages of native peoples in Canada, the U.S., and Mexico, Adams returned to South America in 1919, after the war had ended, to study its indigenous languages. Her quest led her across Chile and then into Argentina, Paraguay, eastern Bolivia, Uruguay, and Brazil. Adams knew that she was gathering more information than she could study in a single lifetime, but she wanted to give something of lasting value to the world, and she believed that this research would do exactly that.

Ultimately, Adams's most valuable contribution did not come from her research. In June 1913, she had been inducted into the Royal Geographical Society, becoming only the third woman—and the first American woman—to receive that honor. Despite her gratitude for this recognition, she could not help feeling angry that women were treated as second-class citizens by the major geographic societies. She had not even been allowed full membership in the National Geographic Society, despite her close association with it. Therefore, Adams made up her mind to found a society especially for women explorers. In 1925, that dream became a reality. The Society of Woman Geographers brought together women from all over the world who traveled extensively to study unique or obscure people, places, and things. The members came from the fields of science, ethnology, archaeology, botany, sociology, the arts, and natural history. In May 1925, Adams was elected the first chair of the Executive Council, and she became the society's first president in December.

Through her exhaustive efforts, Adams built a membership of distinguished women from more than 40 nations. When she stepped down from her presidency in 1933 (to become the honorary president), her fellow women geographers honored her with these words: "[Hers] was not an easy task, mothering and nurturing this group from a tiny nucleus to a widespread organization. . . . But Harriet Adams sent out her own fresh energy and enthusiasm till it vibrated throughout the organization even to its most distant parts, and today the Society of Woman Geographers stands as a monument to her vision, her zeal and her devotion."

Adams presented the Society of Woman Geographers'
first honorary medal to famous aviator Amelia
Earhart in 1933.

In 1926, Adams severely injured her back when she slipped off a cliff during a trip to Spain. Doctors told her she would never walk again—yet by 1928, she was not only walking, but also traveling. Within a year, she visited every country bordering the Mediterranean Sea, including France, Italy, Yugoslavia, Greece, Turkey, Algeria, and Syria. In 1930, traveling by airplane for the first time, Adams fell in love with aviation. She was amazed at how it allowed such rapid movement over vast stretches of land, and she found herself fascinated by the vistas of the earth she gained from high up in the sky. "To see the land from above is to really understand it," she said.

When Frank retired in 1934, the Adamses settled in Europe. Though Harriet intended to focus on her writing, travel continued to lure her away. She still published articles in *National Geographic* and other magazines, but the book she had always wanted to write about her experiences in Peru remained unfinished, a goal to strive toward. When a reporter from the *San Francisco Chronicle* asked her why—of all the places she had visited—she chose to write about Peru, her response came across very clearly: "Perhaps it is because there is hardly a foot of that marvelous land that I have not journeyed over and then, too, Peru is the richest in interest historically." Elsewhere she wrote, "Since the expedition into the inside country of Peru we have reached many other unmapped regions . . . yet no other land has been so dear to me . . . the greatest lure lies in that enchanting forest country on the other side of the Andes."

On July 17, 1937, Harriet Chalmers Adams died in Nice, France. By this time, she was known around the globe as an explorer, a writer, and a humanitarian, though she was most respected in South America, the continent she had loved so deeply. Admirers everywhere noted her concern for indigenous cultures and her promotion of good relations between nations. As a final tribute, the Society of Woman Geographers created the Harriet Chalmers Adams Memorial Endowment Fund, a legacy that would enable more women to succeed in careers of exploration.

As a journalist, spy, and filmmaker, Marguerite Baker Harrison (1879-1967) traveled the world observing the politics, social conditions, and cultural traditions that shape people's daily lives.

4

Marguerite Baker Harrison
The Secret Agent from Baltimore

*O*n a cold night in early 1919, Marguerite Baker Harrison convinced the patrolman on duty at the Brandenburg Gate to allow her to enter Berlin. With his permission, she became the first English-speaking female journalist to reach the city after the armistice that ended World War I. Not even the victorious Allied troops had pressed this far into war-torn Germany. Berlin was still in a state of chaos, with political factions fighting among themselves. Although she anticipated the situation to be dangerous, Harrison in no way expected the barrage of machine-gun fire that overwhelmed her as she and a terrified cab driver hurtled through the darkened streets in a horse-drawn carriage, bullets bouncing on the pavement and ricocheting off the walls of the buildings around them. The cab finally screeched to a halt in front of the Hotel Bristol. Harrison jumped out and paid the driver, who dumped her luggage on the sidewalk and left at a gallop. She hurried to the door, pressing herself as close to the building as possible to avoid stray bullets. At last, the night porter answered the bell, gazed at Harrison in astonished terror, then dragged her inside.

Harrison was traveling undercover as a newspaper correspondent, all the while carrying out intelligence work for the Military Intelligence Division of the United States Army. Though 39 years old at the time, she was new to the life of a secret agent. In fact, given Harrison's privileged and sheltered upbringing, the fact that she became a spy seemed startling, to say the least.

She had been born Marguerite Elton Baker in October 1879 to wealthy American parents whose ancestors had prospered in America since colonial days. Her father, Bernard Nadal Baker, had made his own fortune in Baltimore's thriving shipping trade. Her mother, a member of the venerable Elton family (her first name is unknown), married Bernard at age 18. Marguerite and her younger sister, Elizabeth, grew up like princesses in a 22-room mansion on land inherited by their mother. The girls were cared for by nurses and governesses, and they spent summers voyaging to Europe aboard their father's ships. "By the time I was seven or eight years old I was a seasoned traveler," Marguerite later recalled.

Despite their luxurious life, the Baker family was not a happy one. This was largely due to Marguerite's overprotective mother, who prevented her daughters from forging friendships with other children and offered no real love herself. The two sisters played together, but they were too different to share a close relationship; Elizabeth was shy and cautious, whereas Marguerite was energetic and always ready for adventure. Only with her father did Marguerite share any real companionship, describing her attachment to him as one of "passionate devotion."

Educated at home until age 12, Marguerite began school for the first time in 1891. During her years at the exclusive St. Timothy's School for Girls on the outskirts of Baltimore, she longed for friendships that never materialized. In love with reading, languages, and learning, Marguerite felt painfully different from the other girls. After spending a year at Radcliffe College and then entering Baltimore society as a debutante, Marguerite finally found someone with whom she felt a strong kinship: Thomas Bullitt Harrison, a law student a few years her senior. Despite the protests of her mother, who wanted a more aristocratic husband for her eldest daughter, the two married in 1901. Marguerite gave birth to their son—Thomas Bullitt Harrison II, called Tommy—less than a year later.

The young family lived contentedly in Baltimore for the next 14 years. But when her husband died suddenly of a brain tumor in the spring of 1915, leaving behind a debt of some $70,000, Marguerite's happiness came crashing down around her. Because her husband's debts were professional rather than personal, she was not legally obligated to repay them; nevertheless, she vowed to do so. But she could not turn to her wealthy father, who had suffered devastating financial losses in his steamship line. For the first time, Marguerite Baker Harrison had no one but herself to rely upon. She and a friend ran an interior decorating shop for a time, and Harrison transformed her home into a boarding house to try to make ends meet. Such work did not satisfy her, nor did it bring in enough money, so she decided to supplement her income by writing for the *Baltimore Sun*.

Despite the fact that Harrison had not finished college, could not type, and had never written a news story, the paper's managing editor, Frank Kent, believed she could succeed. Because Harrison was well connected with Baltimore's elite, she was given the job of assistant society editor. She proved to be a talented writer, and Kent soon made her a music and drama critic. In addition, she wrote a weekly column called "Overheard in the Wings" that featured interviews with artists and other celebrities. When the United States entered World War I in 1917, the paper assigned Harrison to cover women's roles in the war effort. Many women had entered the workforce for the first time, filling jobs vacated by men sent overseas to fight. To observe these women in action, Harrison worked as a streetcar conductor and in a steel company shipyard. The experience fueled her confidence in what she could do. In the winter of 1918, with all of Europe at war, Harrison put this realization to the test when she made the radical decision to seek work as a spy for the United States government.

Harrison was inspired by the wartime work performed by women, such as the one shown here manufacturing a rifle at a Pennsylvania factory.

"To this day," Harrison wrote in her autobiography, *There's Always Tomorrow*, "I cannot explain the restlessness that . . . led me to embark on an undertaking that was to change the whole course of my life. . . . I longed to go to France and watch the progress of the war at first hand, but most of all I craved to find out for myself what was going on in Germany. Behind that steel barrier I sensed momentous movements in progress." She was particularly interested in Germany because she had traveled there throughout her childhood and was fluent in the language. She knew the only way to get there during wartime was as a government agent, so she sent an application to General Marlborough Churchill, chief of the army's Military Intelligence Division (MID).

Central to the application was a question that asked, "With what foreign countries and localities are you familiar?" Harrison confidently replied: "The British Isles, France, Holland, Germany, Italy, Austria, Switzerland, Northern Italy, Rome, Naples, Tyrol. I have absolute command of French and German, am very fluent and have a good accent in Italian and speak a little Spanish. Without any trouble I could pass as a French woman, and after a little practice, as German-Swiss. . . . I have been in Europe fourteen times." The MID agent who interviewed her agreed that Harrison was qualified, describing her as "fearless, fond of adventure," and full of "an intense desire to do something for her country."

General Marlborough Churchill (1878-1942) supervised Harrison's career as a spy.

The MID accepted Harrison's application and arranged to send her to Germany. She was initially assigned to report on the German people's attitude toward the war and the possibility of a surrender. Before she could begin her mission, however, the armistice of November 11, 1918, ended the fighting in Europe. Harrison's goal would now be to collect information about political, social, and economic conditions to help the U.S. prepare for the upcoming Paris Peace Conference and determine its future policy toward Germany.

Even though she would not be reporting on top-secret strategic information, Harrison could reveal her mission only to her immediate family and Frank Kent (who assigned her to report on events in Germany for the *Sun* as a cover for her intelligence work). She was well aware of the difficult nature of her job and the danger she faced: "If I succeeded, my efforts would never be publicly recognized. If I failed, I would be repudiated by my government and perhaps lose my life . . . [yet I believed] the risk would be well worth while in view of the possible service I might be able to render our government."

In December 1918, Harrison left her son in the care of friends and set sail for France. From there, she set off via a series of military transports for Coblenz, Germany, headquarters of the occupying U.S. Army. She then ventured beyond her government's protection, arriving in Frankfurt early one January morning "alone on enemy soil—in unoccupied Germany. I had no passes or credentials of any kind. . . . I was uncertain whether I would be allowed to stay." Without any major obstacles, however, she was able to continue on to Berlin by train.

In Berlin, Harrison obtained a Press card from the Foreign Office, enabling her to go anywhere. She also acquired a permit to live in Berlin and a food card, for the Germans were still living on meager war rations. With her link to German newspapers as a journalist, plus letters of introduction to several highly placed people in Berlin, Harrison had little trouble learning about conditions in the city. She cultivated friendships with people from all walks of life—military officers, factory workers, mothers—and saw that most of them were demoralized by the war. While a few Germans lived in luxury, 50 percent were so undernourished that they were close to starvation. Work, fuel, and food were all scarce. Politics were chaotic; militant leftist groups had taken over local governments throughout Germany and were struggling to hold their own against other factions, such as the conservative Pan-Germanists who were determined to restore

An air of despair pervades this street scene in Berlin in June 1919.

the monarchy. Harrison noticed, however, that what the average person talked about was food, not politics.

In addition to writing stories for the *Sun*, Harrison wrote lengthy reports to the MID and dropped them off at the Hotel Adlon for her Berlin contact, Colonel Bouvier, who she rarely met in order to avoid arousing suspicion. As a secret agent, Harrison always worked under the threat of discovery, arrest, and possibly death. But she found that her disciplined, demanding life in Berlin bore little resemblance to the romantic and glamorous image of the female spy in books and movies. She spent her time reading local newspapers, conducting interviews, inspecting factories, and researching statistics. "I rarely had a half-hour to myself during the day," she remembered. "My life was one of continual activity and tension. I was obliged to make and maintain contacts with every political party. I could not afford to overlook any happening great or small that would throw light on conditions in Germany or the secret machinations of this faction or that."

On June 28, 1919, the Paris Peace Conference ended with the signing of the Treaty of Versailles. It contained a clause that declared Germany's expansionist aims had been responsible for the war. The wartime government had been destroyed, yet the treaty held that the German people would still have to pay reparations (payments for damages sustained in war) amounting to some $5 billion. Harrison disagreed with the peace terms, believing that punishing Germany would not help the world recover from the war. She accurately foresaw that the treaty would saddle suffering Germans with further economic hardship, breeding fear and anger that could be manipulated by extremist groups. (German resentment of the Treaty of Versailles did help pave the way for the rise of nationalism, anti-Semitism, and totalitarian government—culminating in the Nazi movement and eventually in World War II.)

Discouraged, Harrison left Berlin and headed back to the United States. Reunited with her son, she initially reveled in her home life. She resumed work at the *Baltimore Sun*, but within a few months she felt sure that this position could no longer satisfy her. She longed to be out in the greater and more dangerous world, and so she contacted General Churchill once again. This time, she proposed operating in Russia as she had in Germany, believing "I could perhaps perform a great service to my country by going to Russia and attempting to secure information that would help our government to formulate some definite policy with regard to the Bolsheviks."

Russia's recent history had been turbulent and—to the outside world at least—mysterious. In March 1917, starving citizens had overthrown the tsar's government. By November, the Bolsheviks (communists) were in power. Their leader, Vladimir Lenin, violently eradicated Russia's imperial past by sanctioning the execution of the tsar and his family, and then set about building a new society in which property was publicly owned and all citizens were equal. Most major countries refused to officially recognize the new government, and Russia cut itself off from contact with the world beyond its borders. As a result, accurate information about Bolshevism or actual conditions in Russia was scarce.

Churchill immediately accepted Harrison's offer, but he cautioned her that she "might be exposed to considerable risks and many hardships." Harrison understood that she would be entering Russia on far shakier grounds than she had entered Germany. She didn't speak the language and had never visited the country. Furthermore, the U.S. government could not offer her an official visa; she would have to manage her entry into Russia on her own. The best credentials she could secure came through the newspapers. Frank Kent, one of only two people in Baltimore who knew the true purpose of her trip, connected Harrison with the Associated Press in London so she could act as its correspondent in Moscow.

Without any legal means of entering Russia, Harrison set sail in November 1919. She took her son with her as far as Switzerland, placing him in a boarding school. Then she left by train for Warsaw, Poland. From there, it took her six weeks to make arrangements to get into Russia. Russia and Poland were at war, and the chaos along the border offered a good chance of slipping into Russia undetected. By crossing the border from Poland, however, Harrison risked being arrested as a Polish spy.

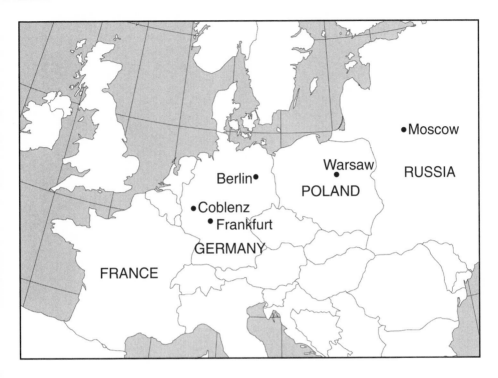

This map shows some of the countries and cities
Harrison visited during her travels as a spy in Europe.

Because of her difficulties with the language, she found a
native Russian speaker, Dr. Anna Karlin, with whom to
make the crossing. In January 1920, with the help of the
Polish military, they set off across the Polish front lines
and no man's land to a village on the Russian front.
Russian officials were completely baffled by the appearance of two women, one of them American, in the middle
of a war zone. Harrison and Karlin spent nearly two
weeks negotiating before they were given permission to
continue by train to Moscow.

"When I arrived in Moscow I knew that I had seen it before," Harrison later wrote of her comfort with and love for the city. "When I talked with the Russians I instinctively understood their point of view."

Once in Moscow, Harrison telephoned immediately to the Russian Foreign Office to announce her arrival, and a government representative was sent to meet her at the station. He was not very happy to see her, for few foreign correspondents were admitted into Moscow. "Do you know that you have done a dangerous and absolutely illegal thing in coming to Moscow without permission?" he demanded. Harrison convinced him to put the matter before his superior, and she was taken to the government guesthouse, more or less under house arrest until the Foreign Office decided what to do with her.

Harrison was allowed to stay on in Moscow for two weeks and eventually for an additional month. Improving her Russian steadily, she visited as many places and took in as many experiences as possible. Each day was filled with trips to schools, nurseries, workmen's clubs, hospitals, and private homes. She interviewed people of all types, including the revolutionary Leon Trotsky, and she heard Lenin give a public speech. What Harrison witnessed fascinated her. "In those days there was something approaching real Communism in Russia," she recalled. All workers were provided with free room and board, and they received their pay in the form of cards entitling them to food, clothing, and other necessities. Harrison did not agree with communism, but she thought it an interesting social experiment that deserved to be tried. She was favorably impressed by the new government, though she also observed some of its problems and limitations. She produced fair, informative articles for the newspapers, but she did not send any intelligence reports for fear she would be discovered. Instead, she committed everything to memory.

Then, one evening as Harrison was walking home, a soldier stopped her on the street and asked for her name. "You're arrested," he told her, handing her the official papers. Astonished, Harrison was taken to Lubianka Prison, where people were imprisoned for political reasons and for espionage. The following morning, a member of the Cheka, the secret police force, told her that she was being held as a spy. He had evidence to prove it—a copy of one of her intelligence reports from Germany, somehow leaked by someone in the MID. He was, however, willing to make a deal. If Harrison would spy on the other foreigners staying in the guesthouse, he would grant her freedom. She accepted his offer, secretly planning to double-cross him while buying enough time to get an underground message to the MID. Although she succeeded in doing so, she knew she was living on borrowed time. Sooner or later, the Cheka would discover what she was up to and come for her again.

As she predicted, on October 24, 1920, Harrison was arrested for a second time and imprisoned in Lubianka. She spent several weeks in solitary confinement in a dark cell before being moved to a small, stuffy room shared with at least seven other women. Eventually, when Harrison became sick with tuberculosis, she was transferred to a better prison to recover. Despite the hardships she endured during her 10 months as prisoner 2961—insufficient food and exercise, filthy conditions, illness, terrible mental strain—Harrison forged sustaining friendships with the other women. To pass the time, they told fortunes, played with cards made out of cigarette papers, sang songs, staged impromptu plays (inventing the dialogue as they went along), and talked with other prisoners via the steam pipes that ran between the cells.

For a while, Harrison believed she would die in prison. As it turned out, however, all American prisoners in Russia were released in exchange for much-needed food supplies from the United States. Harrison was let go in August 1921 and set sail for home. Her imprisonment had been major news in the U.S., but she was dismayed to learn that most people saw her experience as proof of the cruelty of the Russian government. In interviews and lectures, she tried to emphasize that her arrest had been legal and justified, and that she had a tremendous love for Russia and its people. She published two books about her journey, *Marooned in Moscow* and *Unfinished Tales from a Russian Prison*.

The publicity she had gained finished Harrison's career as a secret agent, but this did not put an end to her adventures. Just 10 months after her return from Russia, she traveled to Japan to write a series of magazine articles about conditions in Asia. From Japan, she continued on to Korea, China, and Mongolia, eventually returning to Russia through Siberia. "I did not mind the cold or the discomforts, I was not homesick, lonely, or afraid," Harrison wrote of this period. "This vagabond life had a curious fascination for me." Unfortunately, the Russian government discovered her presence in Siberia and arrested her once again. She was imprisoned in Lubianka for three months before being released, returning home at last in March 1923.

Harrison's vagabond life continued with a trip to the Middle East in April 1924. Along with two other Americans, Merian C. Cooper and a cameraman named

Earnest "Shorty" Schoedsack, she planned to make a travel film. Harrison would appear in the film as well as serving as the film's producer and financial backer; through the help of friends, she had been able to raise $10,000 before leaving the U.S. The trio decided to film the annual overland migration of a little-known nomadic tribe called the Bakhtiari as it moved its herds from winter grazing lands near the Persian Gulf to summer grazing lands in the highlands of central Persia (now Iran). On

On her way to join the Bakhtiari in Persia, Harrison shares a meal of wild goat with inhabitants of Turkey's Taurus Mountains.

this two-to-three-month journey, 5,000 men, women, and children and more than 50,000 livestock had to traverse six mountain ranges and cross dangerous rivers on goatskin rafts. Harrison, Cooper, and Schoedsack ate, slept, and traveled with the tribe while documenting its traditional customs and the challenges of the journey. *Grass*, the film of the migration, premiered in New York the following spring. Although film critics did not know quite what to make of it (since documentary-style films were unknown at the time), geographers praised this visual record of an ancient people's way of life.

During the winter of 1925, Harrison and three other women formed the Society of Woman Geographers, an organization for women who had "blazed new trails in geography, ethnology, natural history, and the kindred sciences." Providing companionship and professional stature to female explorers, scientists, and journalists, the group ultimately grew into an international body with several thousand distinguished members. In 1926, Harrison married English actor Arthur Middleton Blake and settled down to a less adventurous life, though she continued to write. After her husband's death in 1949, however, her wanderlust resurfaced. Among her last journeys was a trip to Berlin after World War II, during which Harrison—now well into her eighties but still as daring as ever—managed to enter the forbidden Communist zone. Marguerite Baker Harrison died on July 16, 1967, at the age of 88.

"The dauntless leader of scientific expeditions into the Arctic, she has captured the spirit of the polar world in photographs of rare beauty," said the American Geographical Society of Louise Arner Boyd (1887-1972) when it gave her its highest award.

5

Louise Arner Boyd
Arctic Pioneer

*O*n the morning of August 3, 1938, the ship *Veslekari* was moored to a field of polar ice along the east coast of Greenland. Good timing and fine weather during the brief Arctic summer had enabled Louise Arner Boyd and her crew to sail farther north than they ever had before. From their stopping point, the North Pole lay just 800 miles away. To the best of Boyd's knowledge, theirs would be the northernmost landing ever made on Greenland's treacherous east coast, where careful navigation of the ice could mean the difference between life and death.

Boyd and the others used a ladder to climb from the ship to the top of the ice that towered 15 feet above. They stumbled across the rough, slippery surface, careful not to break a leg or fall through the cracks in the ice. Then they waded through knee-deep patches of mud as they went ashore. Though they were eager to explore this strange new landscape, the ship's captain insisted that their landing be brief. Winter was approaching, and he didn't dare risk encountering dangerous icebergs on their return voyage. Boyd took full advantage of her few hours on land, snapping hundreds of photographs of the landscape. She knew that she was capturing sights never before recorded on film, and therefore making a vital contribution to the world's understanding of the Arctic.

Once the ship was safely through the ice and well on its way home, Boyd sent a wireless dispatch to the *New York Times* announcing their triumphant landing. On September 9, the *Times* published an article about the voyage, illustrated with a map of the expedition's route and a photograph of Boyd. A member of the American Geographical Society stressed the significance of the event: "Miss Boyd may claim the credit of having gone farther north in a ship along the East Greenland shore than any other American and of having attained what is probably the second highest latitude ever reached by a vessel in these waters."

For Boyd, at the time a veteran of six Arctic expeditions, this accomplishment was the capstone of years of hard work and hard-won experience. The rugged, adventurous field of Arctic exploration might have seemed an unlikely career for a socialite and heiress, but Boyd was a woman of contradictions. At home in her native San Francisco Bay Area, she was one of high society's great ladies. She lived at her family's estate, Maple Lawn, served by a staff of nine. She loved to garden—not in messy gardening clothes, but in a tailored wool suit with a matching hat. She always wore flowers, even on her Arctic voyages; her favorite was the camellia, which she grew in her own greenhouses and wore pinned to her lapel. But despite her love of beautiful things, Boyd did not play the society grande dame on her expeditions. Instead, she wore the gear necessary to endure fierce weather and rugged conditions: oil skins, hip boots, a warm fur hat, and heavy gloves. With dedication and professionalism, she proved she was no rich amateur traipsing through the Arctic on a whim, but an intrepid explorer, a scientist, and eventually a leading expert on this harsh, mysterious region.

Louise was born in San Francisco on September 16, 1887, to John Franklin Boyd and Louise Arner Boyd, who already had two sons. The family was one of the wealthiest and most prominent in the Bay area. Her father had made his fortune in the mining industry, then entered the investment business. During Louise's childhood, the Boyd family divided their time between their house in San Rafael, California, and a horse ranch in the

Left to right: young Louise, her mother, and her brothers, Seth and John

foothills just east of the San Francisco Bay. "I was a tomboy," she recalled. "I rode horseback with my brothers. Often we would pack our saddlebags and ride all day through the hills." Louise was first educated by a series of governesses and later attended private schools in San Francisco.

But in August 1901, Louise's fairy-tale childhood came to an abrupt and painful end when her 17-year-old brother, Seth, died of heart disease. Eight months later, her other brother, 16-year-old John, also died of heart disease. Shocked and grieving, Louise and her parents were always together from that time forward. Both her mother and her father were in poor health, and she vowed to care for them and spend time with them for as long as possible. Louise's father began to involve her in his business affairs, and the family traveled throughout the United States and Europe. When, on one of these trips, Louise decided to take up photography, her parents were supportive of her newfound interest and hired an expert to teach her about lenses, shutter speeds, light, and other technical matters.

In 1919, Louise's mother died. Then her father died a year later, and Louise stepped into his shoes as president of the Boyd Investment Company. At 32 years old, Louise Arner Boyd was entirely alone in the world and an heiress. Like so many other people before her and after, she sought refuge in travel. Accompanied by a friend, she visited France and Belgium, where she was overwhelmed by the recent devastation caused by World War I. She described Europe's ruined cities and burned landscapes in her diary and captured the images of suffering and destruction in photographs.

The next year, Boyd and her friend traveled through Scandinavia, Italy, Portugal, and Spain. The Scandinavian countries woke in her a passion for the north, so in the summer of 1924, she chose a more unusual destination— Spitsbergen, a small group of islands in the Arctic Ocean between Norway and the east coast of Greenland. There,

Boyd caught her first glimpse of the landscape that captivated her throughout her life. "Far north," she wrote, "hidden behind grim barriers of pack ice, are lands that seem to hold one spellbound. . . . One enters another world where men are insignificant amid the awesome immensity of lovely mountains, fiords, and glaciers."

Boyd decided to travel even farther north. Because money was no object for her, she chartered the *Hobby*, a Norwegian seal-hunting ship. Accompanied by a group of friends and a 14-man Norwegian crew, Boyd set sail in the summer of 1926 for Franz Josef Land, a constellation of 70 tiny islands close to the North Pole. "Some American woman wants to see ice," the captain of the *Hobby* had remarked when Boyd hired him. The purpose of the trip was indeed recreational, rather than exploratory. Boyd and her friends hunted polar bears, a common pastime for Arctic travelers at the time. But she also collected plant specimens and photographed the land, sea, and ice. In fact, this first voyage north marked the beginning of Boyd's most important legacy: an immense pictorial documentary of every aspect of the Arctic world. From this point onward, she changed her course in life. "I understood for the first time what an old seaman meant when he told me that once you had been in the Arctic and in the ice, you never could forget it, and always wanted to go back," she wrote. She would return to the Arctic—not as a tourist, but as an explorer, observing and documenting a world few others had experienced.

Boyd poses with a polar bear that she killed on one of her Arctic expeditions. Reports credited Boyd as a skilled hunter who shot as many as 29 bears. She later claimed, however, "it was only five or six and that was for food."

One of the world's least populated areas, the Arctic (the area around the North Pole) had been explored, mostly by Scandinavians, as early as the ninth century. But by Boyd's time, more than 1,000 years later, much was still unknown about the region because its isolation and extreme weather conditions made reaching it so difficult. Before air travel became common, explorers had to make the journey by ship through the Arctic Ocean, which remained largely frozen all year round. Only in the short Arctic summers did the pack ice (large masses of floating

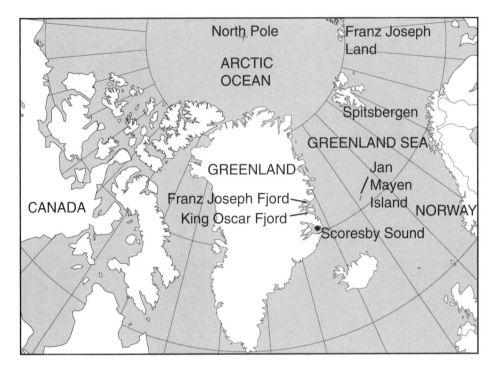

This map of the Arctic shows some of the places Boyd would visit on her many expeditions.

ice covering the ocean) break up enough for ships to pass through. Even then, they often struck pieces of drifting ice and sank, or became trapped in the ice until everyone aboard starved or froze to death. These unpredictable conditions made expeditions long, expensive, and risky. Boyd's love of the region and the finances at her disposal therefore made her an ideal candidate for undertaking Arctic exploration.

In 1928, Boyd chartered the *Hobby* once more, this time with a purpose beyond mere entertainment. She served as expedition leader, carefully planning every detail of the trip, including plotting the ship's course from the northwest coast of Norway to northeastern Greenland. Along with three friends whom she brought along for company, Boyd hired three scientists to map the region, collect samples of plant life, and measure ocean depths. The goals of the voyage changed, however, when Boyd learned that the famous Arctic explorer Roald Amundsen and his airplane were missing. Amundsen had flown north in search of an Italian explorer, General Umberto Nobile, whose hot-air balloon had crashed somewhere in the Arctic. Boyd promptly gave over her ship and crew

Umberto Nobile (1885-1978) was best known for flying across the North Pole with Roald Amundson in the airship Norge—*which Nobile built himself—in 1926. His mascot, a dog named Titina, accompanied him.*

to the government of Norway to help with the search efforts, offering to pay all the costs of the mission.

For three months, the *Hobby* traveled back and forth across the Arctic waters, logging more than 10,000 miles in its quest. During this difficult voyage, Boyd came to appreciate the treachery of the Arctic landscape that so intrigued her. "We would just stand there and look," she said of the search. "Ice does such eerie things. There are illusions like mirages, and there were times we clearly could see tents. Then we'd lower boats and go off to investigate. But it always turned out the same—strange formations of the ice, nothing more." Though Nobile and his crew were rescued by another ship, Amundsen and his crew were eventually given up as lost.

Boyd did manage to shoot several thousand photographs and some 20,000 feet of motion-picture footage detailing the expedition. The search and her role in it made headlines around the world, and she received honors from several governments. Most importantly, she met a number of other Arctic explorers involved in the hunt for Amundsen, and her conversations with them encouraged her to continue her own explorations. All the explorers stressed the need for a good photographer who could take pictures to be used for mapping the region. Boyd knew this was something she could do.

During the summer of 1931, Boyd organized and embarked upon her first major scientific voyage. This time, the ship she chartered was the *Veslekari* and the expedition's destination was the east coast of Greenland, one of the world's largest islands. Except for its coasts, most of Greenland is covered by an ice cap more than two miles thick in some places. The coasts are dramatic and colorful, with snow-covered mountains, high cliffs, and maze-like fjords (long, narrow inlets between rock slopes). Boyd intended to make a preliminary survey of the fjords lying between the 70th and 74th parallels. Along with her maid and her secretary, Boyd again brought a group of friends as passengers.

Several weeks into the expedition, the *Veslekari* anchored in Scoresby Sound, near the only Eskimo settlement in the fjords (also the northernmost settlement on the East Greenland coast). The Eskimos' houses were made of wood and turf with glass windows. Their traditional diet consisted of seal meat, which they hunted from kayaks and dried on high wooden racks. Boyd was impressed by the Eskimos' way of life, as well as by their kindness to her and her fellow explorers. Shortly before the ship departed, the Eskimos came on board for a long farewell. Boyd wrote in her journal that she and the others were "sad to see these splendid, kindly people leave the ship shortly after three o'clock in the morning."

Boyd and her crew covered every part of the region comprising the Franz Josef and King Oscar Fjords. Along the way, she took thousands of photographs and discovered and corrected several errors on existing maps of the area. Most significantly, she discovered a major new glacier

Eskimos had not lived on the East Greenland coast since the 1800s. But in 1925, a 90-member colony of Danish Eskimos settled at Scoresby Sound to help the Danish government establish a claim on the land.

and a previously unknown valley connecting the Kjerulf and Dickson Fjords. Working solely from the 200 photographs Boyd shot during her exploration of these fjords, Dr. Walter A. Wood, a surveyor for the American Geographical Society (AGS), was later able to draw to scale and publish a map illustrating the new connection. Wood's efforts were aided not only by Boyd's excellent camera equipment and use of fine-grain film, but also by her knowledge of photogrammetry, a way of using photography to make precise measurements necessary for drawing maps. In 1932, Boyd was honored to discover that the inner reaches of the fjord she had helped chart had been named "Miss Boyd Land" in her honor.

Perhaps the greatest outcome of the 1931 expedition was the connection Boyd forged with the AGS through its director, Isaiah Bowman. The two spent time together aboard the ship that took Boyd back to the United States from Norway. In long discussions with Bowman, she became intrigued by the AGS's philosophy of integrating many different scientific approaches into its studies. Boyd realized that the AGS could give her the

In 1931, the Danish government named this East Greenland ice formation "Louise Glacier" in honor of Boyd.

credibility she sought as an explorer, while she could be a rich and influential ally for the society. The AGS sponsored and helped to staff Boyd's next three expeditions and published three books by her. She, in return, provided the financial assistance and organizational know-how necessary to make the expeditions work.

Boyd's first joint expedition with the AGS set sail on June 28, 1933. Once again, the ship was the *Veslekari* and Boyd was the expedition leader and photographer. This time, however, she was accompanied by other scientists: a geologist, a physiographer, and two surveyors—one of whom was Walter A. Wood, who had made the map from her photographs. (A botanist was also included, but he had to leave the expedition early in the voyage due to an attack of appendicitis, and Louise took over his work collecting plant specimens.) Their purpose was to study glacial features in the Franz Josef and King Oscar Fjords and chart the northeast coast of Greenland. Boyd sought out the best scientific equipment available for the job, including an ultrasonic depth-measuring instrument that could accurately record the contours of the ocean floor.

The first destination was Jan Mayen Island, midway between Norway and Greenland. Their mission on the island was to deliver mail to the Norwegian government's meteorological station—the first mail the men there had received in close to a year. From there, the most difficult part of the voyage began. In order to reach Greenland, ships had to cross through pack ice, which

The Veslekari *navigates through the Arctic ice.*

could stretch from 100 to 150 miles. No one could predict how long the crossing would take, because the ice changed from year to year. Fortunately, in 1933 the sea was relatively open, and the *Veslekari* was able to cross in about 20 hours. Once they reached the east coast of Greenland, they found the Franz Josef Fjord still closed by ice and had to wait a few days for conditions to change. But by the end of July, Boyd and the scientists were able to go ashore on a glacier, set up camp, and begin their explorations.

The climax of this part of the journey was a three-to-four-week hike across the area known as Fraenkel Land. For all the members of the expedition, elaborate preparations, courage, and endurance were necessary to make the journey on foot across the demanding terrain, which was steep, slippery, and full of boulders. The expedition members had to carry all their gear and scientific equipment on their backs. Boyd's photographic equipment was especially heavy, though she always had at least one assistant to help her carry her camera, tripod, lenses, and

A rare scene of Boyd photographing the Greenland landscape

other supplies. Because time was precious during the brief Arctic summer, the expedition members took full advantage of each day. Despite fine sand that blew into every crevice of her equipment and winds so strong they once knocked her camera down a hill, Boyd worked tirelessly. Since it stayed light nearly all the time in this far northern region, many of her photographs were taken in the middle of the night.

By late August, winter was fast approaching and the group had to leave. Thick fog prevented them from setting sail until September 1. Then, just two days after leaving, the ship ran aground at high tide. Unfortunately, there were no other ships in the area to come to the *Veslekari*'s assistance. If the ship was not released soon, it would be trapped in the ice through the long Arctic winter. As Boyd said, "We were obliged to rely solely on our own resources to get afloat." First, they tried lightening the ship's load to see if the next high tide would free them. When that failed, the ship's captain threw a cable around an iceberg about 700 feet away. The iceberg provided the ship with the necessary leverage to break free of the sticky sediment on the sea floor, and at last, after an extremely difficult start, the *Veslekari* headed out into the open water. As it did, it was hit by blinding snow and 55-mile-per-hour winds. "Nature was closing her doors on us," Boyd concluded.

The result of this rigorous expedition was a book entitled *The Fiord Region of East Greenland*, published by the AGS, coauthored by Boyd and the other scientists, and illustrated with 350 of her photographs. The book also included several maps of photogrammetrical surveys that Boyd had been instrumental in developing, plus maps of the floor of the Greenland Sea.

Boyd made two more Arctic expeditions during the 1930s. In 1937, she discovered an elevated area on the ocean floor near Jan Mayen Island that was later named Louise A. Boyd Bank in her honor. The next year, she made her northernmost landing on the east coast of Greenland. With the outbreak of World War II in 1939, however, Boyd's beloved Arctic became a war zone. Germany conquered Denmark and Norway, gaining control of their territories, which included Greenland and Jan Mayen Island.

A German occupation of Greenland brought the enemy very close to the shores of North America. The United States government desperately needed to acquire Boyd's intimate knowledge of the Arctic to plan a defense against a possible attack. In 1941, she was asked to serve as a consulting expert for the area. She turned over all of her photographs, maps, and notes for the government's use during the war, and in June she went on a military expedition to measure long-distance radio transmission in the Arctic. After the war, she was awarded a Certificate of Appreciation "for outstanding patriotic service to the Army as a contributor to geographic knowledge and consultant."

Showered with awards and honors for her accomplishments as a geographer, Boyd remained active in her sixties and seventies, traveling throughout Asia and the Middle East. She reached the North Pole in June 1955, flying over it as an airplane passenger on what was to be her final Arctic journey. "As I saw the ocean change to massive fields of solid white, my heart leaped up," she wrote. "I knew we were approaching my goal. Then—in a moment of happiness which I shall never forget—our instruments told me we were there. For directly below us, 9,000 feet down, lay the North Pole. . . . We crossed the Pole, then circled it, flying 'around the world' in a matter of minutes. Then we departed. My Arctic dream had come true." The experience showed her how radically exploration had changed: "Land as well as air operations are now on such a vast scale of personnel and equipment, that I am fully cognizant that small expeditions such as mine . . . would be but a dot among the others. . . . We pioneered where others now carry on."

Shortly before her death on September 14, 1972, Boyd asked Walter Wood, the member of the 1933 expedition who had become a lifelong friend, to have her ashes scattered over Greenland. Though political reasons and high costs prevented Wood from fulfilling her request in Greenland, he was able to deliver Boyd's ashes to Alaska—the last northern region she had visited, and an apt resting place for an Arctic pioneer.

"I wanted space, distance, history and danger," said Freya Stark (1893-1993), "and I was interested in the living world." Her passion for knowledge and adventure launched her on a 60-year career of traveling and writing.

6

Freya Stark
Nomad in the Middle East

*I*n 1928, Freya Stark boarded a ship and headed for home. She had just completed her first trip to the Middle East, and its landscapes and cultures had mesmerized her. Now, as Stark stood gazing out at the sea, she made a wish: "How glad I shall be when I can feel that the country is really mine, not the mere panorama of a stranger." More than anything, Stark wanted to feel at home as she traveled abroad, and her curiosity and determination turned this desire into reality. At a time when most Europeans viewed the Middle East as either an exotic mystery or a valuable colonial possession, Stark became intimately acquainted with the Arab world's major cities, seemingly endless deserts, remote villages, languages, religions, history, and wide variety of peoples. As much a writer as she was an explorer, she recorded the experiences of her long nomadic life in 17 history and travel books, 8 collections of letters, and a 4-volume autobiography.

In contrast to her remarkable adventures in later years, Freya Madeleine Stark's early life was far from happy. Her parents, Robert and Flora Stark, were unhappily married British artists living abroad. Freya, their first surviving child, was born in Paris on January 31, 1893. The Starks moved frequently, mostly within England and Italy; Freya later recalled that "our wandering life made us [her and her younger sister, Vera] precocious and pretty tough." The sisters grew up fluent in English, Italian, French, and German, but they did not attend school, and what little education they acquired was from governesses or their own reading. When Freya was 10, her parents separated. Flora and her daughters headed for the grim mountain town of Dronero in the Piedmont region of Italy, where Flora took over the management of a rug and basket factory. This isolated life proved intensely lonely for both girls. Winters were cold, money was tight, their mother was distracted and distant, and they missed their father desperately.

An accident just before Freya's 13th birthday only intensified the problems of an already difficult childhood.

In 1905, during a visit to her mother's factory, a gust of wind blew her thick, knee-length hair into one of the steel looms. Caught in the machinery, Freya was dragged toward the ceiling by her hair. Someone eventually managed to free her, but her scalp and right ear were ripped off in the process. Freya nearly died of an infection before doctors at a hospital in the Italian city of Turin managed to graft skin from her thighs onto her scalp. Though she gradually healed, she remained self-conscious about her disfigurement, covering the right side of her face with her hair. One of Freya's only comforts during her four long months in the hospital was reading. The books she chose transported her to other places, other worlds. Hungering for escape, Freya began reading all she could find about exploration.

In 1912, Freya traveled to London to attend Bedford College, her first formal education. She reveled in this long-awaited opportunity, plunging into the study of English literature and history. The school, however, was forced to close when World War I began in August 1914. Disappointed, Freya packed up and returned to Italy, serving as a nurse during the war years. Afterwards, she and her mother lived in a house on the Italian Riviera, where Freya raised flowers to make ends meet. Living in near poverty, bitter toward her controlling mother, intellectually starved, and yearning for a career as a writer, Freya began to doubt "that I still belong[ed] to the living and thinking world." She sought solace in mountain climbing, scaling the Matterhorn and other peaks in the nearby Alps. And most importantly, she began studying Arabic, first with an old missionary friar and then at the London School of Oriental Studies.

The postwar years had brought a new European interest in the Middle East. With the defeat of the Ottoman Empire (which had covered much of the Middle East, as well as southeastern Europe and northeastern Africa), the victorious British and French gained control of the region. This brought opportunities for Europeans to travel more freely in the area, working as government administrators, making maps, or excavating archaeological sites. Sensing there might be a role for her in these exciting times, Freya Stark learned Arabic "with a hope that it might lead me out [of my old life] into some sort of fairyland of my own."

It was not until November 1927, however, that Stark's dream of adventure came true. With money from some good investments she had made, she boarded a cargo ship headed for Beirut, Lebanon. "It is so wonderful to be away, really away, a new land opening out every morning," she wrote. Arriving in the French-controlled city in early December, Stark traveled high into the hills to the village of Brummana, where she could live with European missionaries while continuing her study of Arabic. Although she had little interest in missionary work, she knew that the familiarity of European language and culture would ease her transition into a land that was so new to her.

In March 1928, feeling more comfortable with speaking Arabic, Stark traveled to Damascus, Syria, the oldest continuously inhabited city in the world. Her extensive reading had led her to believe that Damascus was a romantic oasis on the edge of the desert. She found, however, that modern-day Damascus had poor sanitation, and half the city had been reduced to rubble by the war. It was cold, she was ill with dysentery, and each night she was bitten by the fleas that crawled out of her mattress. Nevertheless, Stark would not let these conditions deter her. One of the seven major rules of travel, according to

Damascus in the late nineteenth century

her, involved separating one's pleasure in a place from one's bodily comfort, and she lived according to her beliefs. She wandered throughout the city's markets and ancient ruins and fell in love with the nearby desert.

Stark's first major adventure was her visit to the region south of Damascus where the Druze tribe lived. The Druze had recently rebelled against French rule, and the French had placed the area under martial law, allowing no travelers to enter. Curious about the mysterious, closed Druze culture, Stark and a British friend slipped across the border. The two women stayed in Druze villages, observing their way of life while trying to evade the French military police. Stark was outraged at the tribe's treatment by the French, who she realized had no intention of allowing the people to govern themselves. After returning to Italy via Jerusalem and Cairo, she wrote an article about the Druze that was published in *Cornhill Magazine* in November 1928. She signed this criticism of French colonial policy with the pen name "Tharaya," which means "She Who Illuminates the World" in Arabic. Publication by a major magazine helped her to believe that she had a real future as a writer, and she went on to write further articles for *Cornhill*.

Satisfied with all that she had learned and experienced, Stark was determined to find a way to return to the Middle East. She could speak excellent Arabic now, and she was hungry for knowledge, exploration, and adventure. By October 1929, she was on her way to Baghdad, the capital of British-held Iraq. Located in the fertile area between the Tigris and Euphrates Rivers, the city was rich in history and full of people from countless cultural and ethnic backgrounds: Arabs, Greeks, Turks, Persians, Jews, Armenians, Assyrians, and Kurds, along with Europeans of many nationalities. Stark found lodgings in an apartment with a view of the Tigris River, where she could look out on the boats carrying merchants, travelers, and pilgrims to and from the city. She bought antiques, visited archaeological sites, and began studying Persian with an old scholar who filled their lessons with stories and folktales.

People of many cultures throng a Baghdad street in 1914.

One of Stark's goals was to track down the ruins of the fortress castles of the Assassins, an ancient religious terrorist sect during the eleventh through thirteenth centuries whose members had mysterious and terrifying ways of infiltrating an area and destroying their enemies. (From their experiences with the Assassins, Europeans had coined the term "assassination.") To find the ruins, Stark consulted a set of German maps from 1835. Then, accompanied by several guides, she headed by mule into

The Rock of Alamut, the site of the Assassins' major fortress, was located high in the mountains and was impossible to reach without a guide. Stark took this picture on her journey in 1930.

the snowcapped Elburz Mountains, where the Assassins had once lived. The journey up the rugged cliffs took 10 days. Along the way, she stayed in small villages where the local people proved very kind, feeding her for little compensation and allowing her to sleep in their huts. Besides visiting several ruin sites, Stark filled in much of the vague information on the British government's maps of the region, adding to the list of mountains and villages. She also corrected a number of errors, including a significant mistake that placed a mountain range on the wrong side of a valley. Upon her return to Baghdad, Stark placed her revised maps in the hands of British intelligence officials. To her enormous delight, they praised her work highly.

Stark made another trip to the Middle East in 1931, staying for nearly two years. She wrote articles for the *Baghdad Times*, ventured back to the land of the Assassins to see more ruins, and studied ancient graves in Luristan (western Iran)—making more improvements to government maps along the way. By the time she returned to Europe, the 40-year-old Stark had begun to build a reputation as an expert on the Middle East. The first great public milestone of her career came soon afterward, when the Royal Geographical Society awarded Stark the Back Memorial Prize. On June 19, 1933, she was honored along with five other explorers in a special ceremony in London. Presenting the prize to Stark, the society's president, Sir William Goodenough, stated, "We recognize that you travel alone with no great regard for your own safety, and without troubling officials too much on that account. We have profited greatly by your literary talent and the attention you have paid to getting accurate . . . names along your routes, contributing to the correctness of our maps." With this official and highly esteemed recognition, Stark found herself in a new stage of her career. Not only would the Royal Geographical Society help her fund future journeys, but her talents and contributions had also been recognized. Her status increased further with the successful publication of her first book, *The Valleys of the Assassins*, in May 1934.

Stark spent that summer preparing for another journey to the Middle East, poring over ancient maps as well as contemporary ones. The object of her quest was Shabwa, a legendary place believed to have been a trading center from the beginning of civilization. Every explorer who came to the part of the southern Arabian Peninsula that is now Yemen dreamed of finding Shabwa, but none had ever reached the buried city. People believed the site lay deep in the desert in the extreme western corner of the Wadi Hadhramaut, the most fertile valley in the area. Two rival tribes occupied the Hadhramaut, the Qu'aiti and the Kathiri, and warfare between the groups made travel in this area dangerous and difficult.

Adding to the challenge was the fact that Yemen had been divided into two parts. The south was British territory, but the north was an independent kingdom whose ruler (known as an imam) was fiercely hostile to

European influence. To reach Shabwa, Stark would have to slip undetected across the border into the imam's land. She believed that if she could do so, she would find at least some part of the treasure said to be buried at Shabwa. "No one has been anywhere *near* where I want to get, as far as I know, and there must be masses of old ruins strewn all over the countryside," she wrote to a friend.

In November 1934, Stark traveled by ship to Aden, the capital of British Yemen. In mid-January, she set off by donkey for the Hadhramaut, with two Bedouin tribesmen as guides. A nomadic desert people, the Bedouin made ideal guides for Stark's expedition. Though she had some trouble understanding their Arabic dialect, Stark got along well with them. She liked people of all kinds, and she always tried to fit into any given situation. She shared their meals of rotting fish—often shark meat—and rice, and this pleased the two Bedouin greatly.

Unfortunately, when Stark and her guides reached the village of Masna'a, they found themselves in the midst of a measles epidemic. Stark caught the disease almost immediately. She lay on a pallet for more than a week, delirious and dirty, for the local people believed that it was dangerous to wash while ill. Stark eventually became well enough to travel, and by mid-February, she and her guides reached Seiyun, a medieval town surrounded by farms. From there, she explored the Hadhramaut, staying in villages where she found unique towers that rose to great heights, their tops adorned with ibex horns and

The Wadi Hadhramaut, photographed by Stark in 1935. The architecture of the region consisted of tall towers that resemble modern-day skyscrapers.

ornamental designs. But before she could reach the desert where Shabwa lay, Stark again fell ill. Believing herself to be sick with malaria, she began taking another medication on top of the medicine she used to treat dysentery, which caused her to suffer a heart attack. Through sheer luck, a pharmacist happened to be in the area and was able to treat her in the nick of time, saving her life. Stark sent to Aden for help and, 10 days later, four Royal Air Force bombers arrived with a doctor who decided that she must return to Aden and be hospitalized at once.

The sickness had ended Stark's dream of discovering Shabwa. Even as she lay ill, a German photographer found the fortress ruins, though he was chased off by angry tribesmen before he could explore them. A year later, an Englishman named Harry St. John Philby became the first European to enter Shabwa. But Philby made the trip neither on foot nor on the back of a donkey; instead, he traveled by car, a fact that horrified Stark. Fortunately, Philby realized that Stark had helped pave the way for him, and he gave her public credit in his book *Daughters of Sheba* (1940). Meanwhile, stories of Stark's adventures began to spread rapidly. The international news dramatized her journey, dubbing her "one of our most daring young explorers." The book she published about the expedition, *The Southern Gates of Arabia* (1936), became a bestseller. And in 1937, she returned to the Hadhramaut as the leader of an archaeological team to study other ruins she had found on her journey—the first excavation ever made in Yemen.

In January 1939, Stark undertook a very different kind of job. World War II had begun, and the British Ministry of Information offered her a post as a South Arabia expert in Aden. Stark's goal there, and later in Cairo and Baghdad, was to help find a way to keep Arabs neutral or allied with the British—rather than supporting the fascist Italians or Germans—during the war. Her

Freya Stark poses in the traditional costume of the Hadhramaut region of Yemen.

first mission was a dangerous one: to venture into the closed territory of northern Yemen, assess the Italian influence there, and find out where the imam's loyalties lay. She brought with her a film projector to show propaganda movies about Britain's culture and military might. Lodged with the women in the imam's harem, Stark was able to discover a great deal of secret information, and—

though officially forbidden by the imam—the films she showed were popular. It was to Stark's credit that Yemen ultimately remained neutral in the war. When she transferred to Cairo and then Baghdad, she worked to organize and recruit Arab members for an anti-fascist, pro-democracy group called the Ikwan al-Hurriyah (Brotherhood of Freedom). The group proved successful, claiming 78,000 members by 1947.

Stark addresses members of the Brotherhood of Freedom in Cairo in 1940. Modeled after secret societies Arabs had created to resist British rule, the Brotherhood was organized into cells (small groups) and reached out to all levels of society.

When the war ended in 1945, Stark returned to her home in the Italian town of Asolo. She found that her house had been forcibly occupied by fascist leaders during her absence and the surrounding countryside was devastated. Her life, too, had been changed by the war. Previously she had been known as a traveler and writer, but now she was a public figure, famous throughout Europe and the Arab world as a friend to government officials, military leaders, and socialites alike. Stark's life changed still further in 1947, when she married Stewart Perowne, a British official she had worked with in Aden. The marriage was unhappy almost from the start, however, and by 1952 the two had separated.

For the next 30 years, Stark devoted herself to writing. She published her autobiography and nearly a dozen more travel books, all of which proved enormously popular with their blending of history, archeology, travel, and personal essay. In the 1950s, Stark traveled widely through Turkey, which fascinated her with its rich history as one of the centers of classical civilization. Her experiences in Turkey inspired four books, illustrated with her own photographs, about her visits to ancient Greek ruins and her journey retracing the path of Alexander the Great's army. Another major travel book was *The Minaret of Djam* (1970), which recounted her excursion into a nearly inaccessible part of Afghanistan at the age of 75. In 1972, she was knighted for her many achievements by the Queen of England, becoming Dame Freya Stark.

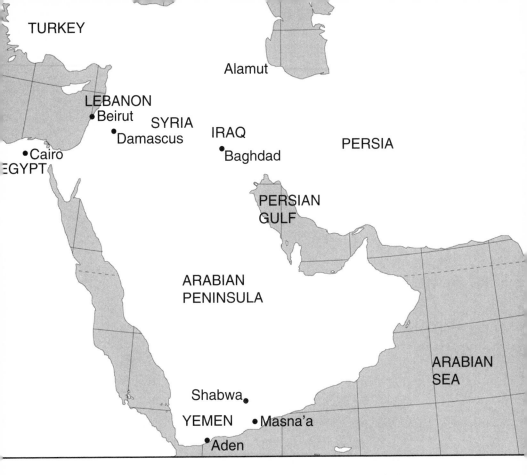

A map of the Middle East, labeled with some of the places Stark visited

Unafraid of change and passionate about exploration, Stark continued to travel throughout the Far East, Persia, Central Asia, India, and North Africa until she was 90 years old. She died at the age of 100 in May 1993. Even the threat of death had not daunted her, however, for she viewed it as only travel of a different kind. "Waiting for death, my dear," she had told a friend, "is very much like being in an old-fashioned steam train, setting out on a journey."

131

The first woman to travel across the ice to both the North and South Poles, Ann Bancroft (b. 1955) continued the tradition of exploration into the twenty-first century.

7

Ann Bancroft
To the Ends of the Earth

*A*t the brink of an open gap in the ice, Ann Bancroft suddenly dropped from sight. The snow she stood on had given way, plunging her into the freezing Arctic Ocean. Luckily, she extended her arms just in time to keep herself from going fully underwater. Bancroft quickly wriggled up over the edge, but she wasn't out of danger yet. She was soaking wet up to her waist, a potentially deadly condition when the temperature outdoors was 30 degrees Fahrenheit below 0. She hurried back to her companions, who frantically searched for dry clothes as Bancroft stripped off her wet pants and socks. Not one to complain, she dressed quickly and got back to work pulling and pushing the sleds forward, raising her body temperature with the exercise. She calmly accepted the experience as just another day in the life of a polar explorer. Still, it took two days for her to feel warm again.

The only woman in the eight-member Steger International Polar Expedition, Bancroft was determined to be the first woman to travel by dogsled to the North Pole. Two other explorers had been forced to leave the expedition early due to injuries. But having dreamed of polar exploration since she was a child, Bancroft didn't want to give up. Her courage and resolve not only ensured her success on the Steger Expedition, but also drove her to become a leader of future expeditions and a role model for the thousands who followed the news of her adventures to the ends of the earth.

Ann Bancroft was born on September 29, 1955, in Mendota Heights, Minnesota, to Richard and Deborah Bancroft. Ann got an early start on exploring the world, spending fifth and sixth grades living with her family in Kenya, Africa. Camping and canoeing trips with her parents in the wilderness of northern Minnesota bred in her a love for the outdoors, and she became an expert backpacker, skier, and mountaineer. A strong athlete, she also excelled at school sports, including basketball and tennis. At the age of 12, she became fascinated by Alfred Lansing's book *Endurance*, which chronicled the amazing survival story of Antarctic explorer Ernest Shackleton. She began learning about other famous explorers and far-away places, dreaming of making long expeditions herself.

Ann's indoor life was not as easy. "School was always pretty iffy for me, because I'm dyslexic," she later recalled. Her learning disability made reading and retaining information difficult. Ann struggled through school and was relieved to earn her high-school diploma. She went to the University of Oregon to become a teacher, hoping to help other students find confidence in athletics and overcome challenges as she had. The university, however, almost barred her from the teaching program because she didn't have the minimum grades. Her college advisor suggested that she quit athletics to devote more time to studying, but Ann refused, certain that "a part of my spirit would die if I quit sports." She continued to play, overcame the education department's objections, and graduated with a degree in physical education and special education.

Bancroft taught in Minneapolis-St. Paul schools and continued her outdoor expeditions, which included climbing Alaska's Mount McKinley (the tallest peak in North America) in 1983. In the summer of 1985, explorer Will Steger contacted her about a dogsled expedition he was planning to the North Pole. He had seven men ready to go, but they needed one more person. Steger had heard about Bancroft's expert rescue of a partner who suffered from hypothermia while climbing Mount McKinley. Even though she had no Arctic experience and had never dogsledded before, he was impressed enough with her outdoor skills to invite her to join his expedition. Since no woman had yet traveled across the ice to the North Pole, Steger knew that Bancroft's presence would bring a great deal of support and publicity to his expedition. She jumped at the chance, saying "Count me in!"

In October, Bancroft joined Steger and the other explorers in northern Minnesota to train for the trip. By the end of the winter, she had learned the art of dogsledding. She got along well with the dogs and her fellow explorers, winning respect with her positive attitude and ability to learn quickly. Both these qualities would be important assets in the 1,000-mile journey across the frozen Arctic Ocean from the Northwest Territories in Canada to the North Pole.

Although explorers had reached the Pole before, most had done so by picking up food and other supplies dropped by airplanes along the way. The Steger Expedition would be different; it would rely only on the power of people and sled dogs, carry everything it needed, and accept no outside help. It was a deliberate return to the days of the early explorers, the first trip of its kind since Robert Peary's famous expedition in 1909. The explorers had to pack carefully to make sure they had enough supplies to survive until they reached the Pole, but not so many that the sleds would be impossibly heavy. And they would need to maintain a steady pace on the journey, or their food would run out.

On March 8, 1986, the Steger Expedition—eight people, forty-nine dogs, and four sleds—set out from the Northwest Territories. Their first task was to cross the frozen Arctic coastline, a rough border of ice chunks ranging in size from boulders to small buildings. Progress was painfully slow. In temperatures that reached 70 degrees below 0, the explorers hacked through chunks of ice, carving a path for the 16.5-foot-long, 1,350-pound sleds. Then the dogs pulled the sleds along the open path while

Paul Schurke and Ann Bancroft guide their sled dogs across a lead (a gap in the ice), one of the many kinds of difficult Arctic terrain the Steger Expedition faced.

Bancroft and the others pushed from behind. In the first day, the expedition covered only one and a half miles.

To protect themselves from the bitter cold, the explorers wore layers of clothing covering every inch of their bodies. They even wore parkas, hats, and mittens inside their tents and sleeping bags at night. After a long day of sledding, they would feed the dogs and tie them to stakes outside the tents so they wouldn't fight or wander away. Then they made dinner for themselves, cooking over small gas stoves. Because keeping body temperature high in the extreme cold requires lots of energy, they had to consume three times the normal amount of calories, which meant eating high-fat foods like pemmican (dried meat), cheese, butter, peanut butter, and energy bars. In their downtime, the explorers discussed the day's progress, took photographs, cared for the dogs, wrote in their journals, mapped out their trail, and recorded data about their physical and mental health for scientific studies. Bancroft and the others were always grateful to have chores to keep them moving and thus keep them warm.

The cold, harsh conditions took their toll on everyone. Most suffered from frostbite, which turned patches of skin black on faces, fingers, and toes. Two explorers, Bob McKerrow and Bob Mantell, eventually had to be airlifted off the trail due to severe injuries—McKerrow had some broken ribs, and gangrene threatened Mantell's frostbitten toes. These two had been Bancroft's closest friends in the group, and she found herself increasingly lonely after their departure. Every time she felt discouraged, however, Bancroft drew on her school experiences to fuel her determination. "When I was having a bad day on the Arctic ice," she remembered, "that's what I would dredge up in my mind to keep me going: *School was harder*."

In the fifth week of the trip, Steger broke bad news to the remaining expedition members: they were moving slower than planned, food rations were running low, and at the rate they were going, they wouldn't have enough food for all the explorers to make it to the North Pole. He proposed that only two or three members should go the rest of the distance, and the others should be airlifted home. This would allow the expedition to succeed even if every member did not make it to the Pole. The explorers were disappointed and angry. Feeling that it was too early to airlift anyone out, Bancroft and another team member suggested an alternate plan that would delay sending anyone home and hopefully allow more explorers to reach the Pole. The team adopted this new approach, and all six remaining members continued on.

After discarding excess equipment on the trail, the expedition hit an area with an expanse of smooth ice. They traveled 20, 25, then 35 miles a day. The dogs' spirits soared and they ran faster. Temperatures reached 15 degrees below 0, warm for the Arctic. A problem with their navigation device turned into good luck when it led the team to circumvent a large break in the ice that could have ended their trip. On May 1, 1986, six frostbitten, coughing, tired explorers arrived at the North Pole. Since the Pole is located in an area covered with drifting ice, no monument marks the exact spot, and they had to figure their position with navigation equipment before they realized they had made it. The next day, photographers and journalists arrived by plane to record the triumphant moment. After a quick celebration, the explorers and their dogs flew back to Minnesota, leaving the solitude of the ice and entering the media's spotlight.

At the North Pole, from left to right: Will Steger, Paul Schurke, Ann Bancroft, Brent Boddy, Geoff Carrol, and Richard Weber

The National Geographic Society, which had sponsored the expedition, featured the team in its magazine, highlighting Bancroft as the only woman on the trip. Television networks offered her jobs as a commentator. Several men proposed marriage to her without even meeting her! But Bancroft had other plans. She returned home with a new dream combining her two passions, exploration and education. She wanted to lead the first all-women's expedition across Antarctica, the coldest, driest, windiest, most remote place on Earth. She would design the expedition to help schoolchildren learn about the continent while motivating them to achieve their dreams. Bancroft founded a nonprofit organization called the American Women's Trans-Antarctic Expedition (AWE) to plan and raise money for the journey, which would extend from one end of Antarctica to the other, crossing the South Pole. She wanted to go with three other women during the months of November through February (summer in Antarctica, which is in the Southern Hemisphere). The women would ski, towing supplies on sleds and being resupplied by airplane.

Explorers usually seek funding for their expeditions from large corporations because training, travel, supplies, and equipment are so expensive. Adding up all the costs, Bancroft estimated she needed $1 million. But although AWE contacted hundreds of companies, none offered financial support. Bancroft suspected they were worried that a women's expedition would not receive enough media attention, or that it would fail and reflect badly on its sponsors. "Get a man involved and then come talk to me," one potential sponsor told her. Discouraged, Bancroft turned to grassroots support from individuals, mainly schoolchildren, teachers, and parents. "We sold T-shirts and posters to get to the South Pole," she said. After four years, AWE finally raised the money to start the expedition, though not enough to pay off all its debts. All Bancroft could do was hope that once the expedition was underway, it would gain more media coverage and interest more donors.

While struggling to fund the expedition, Bancroft looked for explorers to accompany her. She eventually settled on Sue Giller and Anne Dal Vera, both of whom had extensive wilderness experience. To test equipment, get in shape, and learn to work as a team, Bancroft, Giller, and Dal Vera went on two training trips in places with conditions similar to those of Antarctica—first the Northwest Territories of Canada and then Greenland, which they crossed in a 300-mile, six-week trek in 1992. Filling the spot vacated when another explorer backed out, Sunniva Sorby became the fourth member of the expedition less than a month before departure, missing both training trips.

In autumn 1992, the four women left Minnesota for Punta Arenas, Chile, one of the closest places to Antarctica. After a frustrating two-week weather delay, they boarded a plane on the only airline that flew to Antarctica. Finally, on November 9, 1992, the expedition

AWE members haul their sleds as they ski across the snow.

arrived at Hercules Inlet on the northwestern coast of Antarctica. The next day, with their 200-pound sleds in tow, they glided off on skis over the hard-packed snow.

As the days passed, the women settled into a routine. They awoke around 6:00 A.M., had breakfast, packed up their camp, and hit the trail by 9:00 A.M. They would ski for about two hours, take a break for snacks or lunch, and then start again, traveling four to fifteen miles on most days. Sometime between 6:30 and 8:00 P.M., the explorers stopped for the day, set up their two tents, and took turns cooking dinner. They ate a variety of high-energy foods, including butter, cheese, meat, oatmeal, hash browns, rice, beans, and pasta. Before bedtime (between 10:00 and 11:00 P.M.), they mended clothes, tended to injuries, and plotted their course using a Global Positioning System (GPS)—a computerized device that received data on their location, mileage, elevation, and direction from satellites in space. The women also took psychological tests for a University of Minnesota study on extreme stress, and they collected samples of their saliva so that doctors could later study the effects of the expedition on their health. In addition, Bancroft called in reports by radio to AWE headquarters. From these reports, AWE created e-mails and recorded telephone messages that allowed more than 250,000 schoolchildren in the United States and Canada to follow the expedition's progress.

The expedition members were resolved to work hard, but above all, they wanted to strengthen their friendships, have fun, and enjoy Antarctica. "It's beautiful and I love it," Bancroft wrote in her journal. "This feels more profound than anything I've done. More amazing. I've wanted to do this for so long. Put together the project—lead it—do it." She strove to be a good leader, pushing the team to travel as far as possible each day while trying to ensure their health and safety. All four explorers were struggling with the cold and with skiing-related injuries. Bancroft had frostbite, Giller and Dal Vera had tendinitis in their ankles, and Dal Vera also experienced depression. Sorby, however, suffered the worst, with a sprained ankle and severe bronchitis. As her symptoms worsened, she couldn't pull as much weight on her sled, and the other three women had to tow some of her gear. Unable to endure long days of travel, Sorby struggled to find the strength to persevere.

As the situation worsened, the group made a difficult decision. Because of Sorby's injuries and Dal Vera's physical and emotional state, Bancroft asked the two to think about leaving the expedition at the South Pole, the midpoint of their trip. Frustrated and sad, Dal Vera and Sorby agreed. Bancroft now worried whether the group could even make it to the Pole. If Sorby collapsed, the other women, tired from the long journey, might not have the strength to carry her—and a rescue plane could not land in their current location. All the explorers could do was reduce their skiing hours and hope that Sorby recovered.

After a number of shortened days, they reached the Pole on January 14, 1993. As the four skiers approached, residents came out to cheer them on and film their arrival. (The South Pole has a research station inhabited by scientists from around the world.) Together, Bancroft, Giller, Dal Vera, and Sorby touched the South Pole, marked by a large pole with a silver globe on top. They were the first women to reach the Pole on foot. In addition, Bancroft was the first woman to cross the ice to both the North and South Poles.

Once safely at the Pole, Bancroft struggled to decide about the rest of the expedition. Because of the delays in

(From left to right) Ann Bancroft, Anne Dal Vera, Sunniva Sorby, and Sue Giller celebrate their triumphant arrival at the South Pole.

Punta Arenas and in their trek to the Pole, less time was left for the second half of the trip. She and Giller would have to make fast progress to reach the other side of the continent in time to catch a ship home. If they missed the ship, they would have to pay an extra $350,000 for an airplane flight out of Antarctica. Because of the debt the AWE had already incurred and the spirit of teamwork and support the expedition embodied, Bancroft decided that it would not be right to go on without the whole group. She had organized the trip "not to make the Pole—but to work as a team—travel as a team." The explorers ended their trek at the South Pole, after traveling 660 miles in 67 days.

For several years after the expedition, Bancroft worked hard to pay off AWE's debt through speaking engagements and fundraisers. AWE was eventually converted into the Ann Bancroft Foundation, giving grants to support the achievements of girls and women. Bancroft was profiled in magazines, newspapers, and radio and television programs, and in 1995 she was inducted into the National Women's Hall of Fame. As time passed, she yearned to return to the Antarctic ice to complete her trek: "I had to go back. It's what I've been wanting to do since I was twelve." So Bancroft started planning another ski expedition across Antarctica. She would go with just one companion, 47-year-old Liv Arnesen from Norway.

Bancroft tried something different this time: she founded a for-profit organization, yourexpedition, that employed marketing and public relations professionals to raise money for the trip. This time, she managed to pay for the entire $1.5 million expedition before leaving, thanks to sponsorships from major corporations like Volvo, Pfizer, and Motorola. This funding allowed the Bancroft Arnesen Expedition to utilize cutting-edge technology. Besides navigating with GPS, the explorers would use satellite phones, digital cameras, and laptop computers to communicate with the rest of the world. Their journal entries, voice messages, and photographs would be published daily on a web site where people could check their progress and even send e-mails to the explorers. Bancroft also developed an Antarctica curriculum that would be published on the Internet, reaching three million schoolchildren. In the coming months, people from 116 countries followed along with the expedition on the web site and in the media.

After a two-week weather delay in Cape Town, South Africa, Bancroft and Arnesen slapped skis down

Bancroft and Arnesen used sails to help pull their sleds over the snow.

on the Antarctic snow on November 14, 2000. Each woman pulled a 260-pound sled. They had sails to help carry them on days when the wind was blowing steadily; once attached to the sleds, the sails would fill with wind, extend into the sky like parachutes, and pull the explorers and their sleds along. Their route stretched from Queen Maud Land, the part of Antarctica just south of South Africa, across the continent to McMurdo Station on the Ross Ice Shelf (the ice beyond the edge of the Antarctic landmass). They would cross mountains, glaciers, and the South Pole. The women planned to pick up fresh supplies at the South Pole and then continue on from where Bancroft's last expedition left off.

After 64 days, on January 16, 2001, Bancroft and Arnesen reached the South Pole. Along the way, they had been frustrated by unusually windless weather that made their sails useless, delaying their progress. They now had just until February 22 to reach the coast, where a ship would pick them up. The pair bathed, ate, rested briefly, and headed out again. They made a grueling climb up the 10,200-foot Titan Dome, then a steep descent down the jagged ice of the Shackleton Glacier. On the Ross Ice Shelf, the expedition again stalled because of windless days. Bancroft and Arnesen knew they had little hope of covering the remaining 500 miles without using their sails, and so they made the difficult decision not to finish their planned route. On February 18, they were airlifted to McMurdo Station. They hadn't accomplished as much as

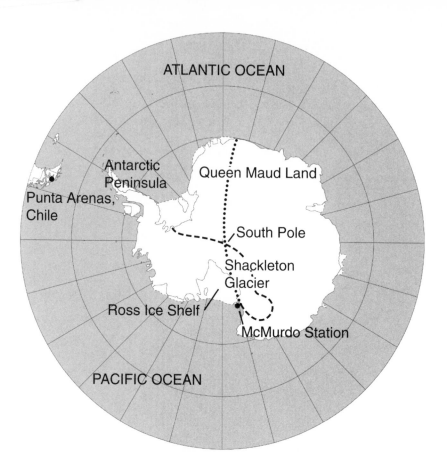

The planned routes of the AWE (dashes) and the Bancroft Arnesen Expedition (dots)

they planned, but in their 94-day, 1,717-mile trek they had still crossed the entire Antarctic landmass (since the Ross Ice Shelf is not technically land), becoming the first women to do so. Though she was disappointed, Bancroft believed that "there is value to ending like this because you can teach kids that you don't always get all the pieces of the dream. The important ones are those that you do get."

Bancroft continued to seek out more pieces of her dream journey. In January 2002, she and Arnesen returned to Antarctica to celebrate the anniversary of their expedition. They kayaked around the Antarctic Peninsula, the part of the continent nearest to Argentina. From there, they announced another expedition: a 1,790-mile trip through the Great Lakes by kayak and other forms of water transportation. In contrast to the isolation of a polar expedition, this May 2002 trip allowed Bancroft and Arnesen to meet their supporters face to face. Most importantly, the explorers demonstrated that adventure can happen anywhere, not just at the ends of the earth.

Liv Arnesen (left) and Ann Bancroft, shown here at the South Pole, remained good friends after their trip and planned to continue their adventures together.

Bibliography

Adams, Harriet Chalmers. "Along the Old Inca Highway." *National Geographic*, April 1908.

———. "Some Wonderful Sights in the Andean Highlands." *National Geographic*, September 1908.

"After North Pole Conquest, Explorers Head Back." *Philadelphia Inquirer*, May 4, 1986.

Anema, Durlynn. *Harriet Chalmers Adams: Adventurer and Explorer*. Greensboro, N.C.: Morgan Reynolds, 1997.

———. *Louise Arner Boyd: Arctic Explorer*. Greensboro, N.C.: Morgan Reynolds, 2000.

"Antarctic White-Out Delays Skiers' Plane." *Philadelphia Daily News*, February 16, 2001.

Boyd, Louise Arner. *The Fiord Region of East Greenland*. American Geographical Society, 1935.

David-Neel, Alexandra. *My Journey to Lhasa*. Boston: Beacon, 1986.

Foster, Barbara and Michael. *Forbidden Journey: The Life of Alexandra David-Neel*. New York: Harper & Row, 1987.

———. *The Secret Lives of Alexandra David-Neel: A Biography of the Explorer of Tibet and its Forbidden Practices*. Woodstock, N.Y.: Overlook, 1998.

"Four Women on a Test of Will in Antarctica All Will Pull Sleds of Food and Supplies Weighing Almost Twice Their Body Weights. Then There is the Bitter Cold." *Philadelphia Inquirer*, October 25, 1992.

Frank, Katherine. *A Voyager Out: The Life of Mary Kingsley*. Boston: Houghton Mifflin, 1986.

Geniesse, Jane Fletcher. *Passionate Nomad: The Life of Freya Stark*. New York: Random House, 1999.

Glynn, Rosemary. *Mary Kingsley in Africa*. London: Harrar, 1956.

Harrison, Marguerite. *There's Always Tomorrow: The Story of a Checkered Life*. New York: Farrar & Rinehart, 1935.

"'I've Been Trying to Do This for 11 Years,' One Said. In a First, Two Females Ski Across 1,800 Miles of Frozen Antarctica." *Philadelphia Inquirer*, February 13, 2001.

Loewen, Nancy, and Ann Bancroft. *Four to the Pole!: The American Women's Expedition to Antarctica, 1992-1993*. North Haven, Conn.: Linnet, 2001.

Martin, Katherine. *Women of Courage: Inspiring Stories from the Women Who Lived Them*. Novato, Calif.: New World Library, 1999.

Miller, Luree. *On Top of the World: Five Women Explorers in Tibet*. Paddington Press, 1976.

Olds, Elizabeth Fagg. *Women of the Four Winds: The Adventures of Four of America's First Women Explorers*. Boston: Houghton Mifflin, 1985.

Ruthven, Malise. *Traveller through Time: A Photographic Journey with Freya Stark*. New York: Viking, 1986.

Stark, Freya. *The Zodiac Arch*. London: John Murray, 1968.

Steger, Will, and Paul Schurke. *North to the Pole*. New York: Random House, 1987.

Stiever, Greg. *Poles Apart*. Lead Dog Productions, 2000. Documentary film.

Tinling, Marion. *Women into the Unknown: A Sourcebook on Women Explorers and Travelers*. New York: Greenwood, 1989.

yourexpedition website. www.yourexpedition.com.

Index

Adams, Frank (husband), 58, 60, 61, 62, 63-65, 67, 73

Adams, Harriet Chalmers: books and articles written by, 66, 73; death of, 73; early years of, 59-60; and founding of Society of Woman Geographers, 13, 71; interest of, in Native American origins, 67-69, 70; miscellaneous travels of, 67, 68-69, 72; relationship of, with National Geographic Society, 66, 71, 73; as speaker, 66, 67, 70; travels of, in Latin America, 13, 56, 57-59, 60, 61, 62, 63-65, 67, 70; travels of, in Peru, 58, 63-64, 73; as war correspondent, 69-70

Aden, 125, 126, 127, 130

Afghanistan, 130

Africa, 9, 12, 19; European colonies in, 20, 33; Kingsley in, 13, 16, 17-18, 22-27, 29-33; people of, 21, 23-24, 27, 29, 30-31, 32-33; religions of, 25, 27, 28, 33

African Society, 35

Akeley, Delia, 12

Alexander the Great, 130

American Fund for French Wounded, 69

American Geographical Society (AGS), 94, 96, 106, 107-108, 112

American Women's Trans-Antarctic Expedition (AWE), 141-142, 143, 144, 146, 147, 150

Amundsen, Roald, 103, 104

Andes Mountains, 57, 58, 63, 64, 65

Angola, 24

Ann Bancroft Foundation, 147

Antarctica, 14, 141; Bancroft in, 14, 142-147, 148-151

Arctic, 101-102; Bancroft in, 133-134, 136-140; Boyd in, 13, 14, 94, 95-97, 100, 101, 102-107, 108-111, 112, 113

Arctic Ocean, 99, 101-102, 133, 136

Arequipa, 63, 64

Army, U.S., 76, 82

Arnesen, Liv, 147, 148-151

Assassins, 122-123

Atkinson, Lucy, 9

Back Memorial Prize, 123

Baghdad, 120-121, 123, 127, 129

Baghdad Times, 123

Baker, Bernard Nadal (father of Harrison), 76, 77, 78

Baker, Elizabeth (sister of Harrison), 76-77

Baker, [first name unknown] Elton (mother of Harrison), 76, 77

Bakhtiari tribe, 92-93

Baltimore Sun, 78, 79, 82, 84, 85

Bancroft, Ann: Antarctic expeditions of, 14, 142-151; as athlete, 134, 135; AWE established by, 141-142, 146, 147; and Bancroft Arnesen Expedition, 147-150; early years of, 134-135; North Pole reached by, 14, 132, 134, 140, 145; South Pole reached by, 14, 15, 132, 145, 149, 151; in Steger Expedition, 133-134, 136-

140; as teacher, 14, 15, 135, 141, 148

Bancroft, Deborah (mother), 134

Bancroft, Richard (father), 134

Bancroft Arnesen Expedition, 147-150

Batanga, 29

Bedouin tribes, 10, 125

Berlin, 75-76, 82-84, 93

Bishop, Isabella Lucy Bird, 10-11

Blake, Arthur Middleton (second husband of Harrison), 93

Blunt, Anne, 9-10

Boddy, Brent, 140

Boer War, 35

Bolsheviks, 85, 86

Bouvier, Colonel, 84

Bowman, Isaiah, 107

Boyd, John (brother), 97, 98-99

Boyd, John Franklin (father), 97, 99

Boyd, Louise Arner: Arctic explorations of, 13, 14, 94, 95-97, 100, 101, 102-107, 108-111, 112, 113; awards and honors of, 94, 104, 106-107, 112-113; books written by, 108, 111-112; death of, 113; early years of, 97-99; expeditions of, to Greenland, 95-96, 105-107, 108-111, 112; as photographer, 13, 94, 96, 99, 100, 104, 105, 106, 108, 110-111, 112; relationship of, with American Geographical Society, 107-108, 112

Boyd, Louise Arner (mother), 97, 98, 99

Boyd, Seth (brother), 97, 98

Boyd Investment Company, 99

Brandenburg Gate, 75

British Museum, 28

Brotherhood of Freedom, 129

Bubi tribe, 29

Buddhism, 40, 42, 43, 44, 48, 54

Burton, Richard, 20-21

Cabinda, 25

Cairo, 120, 127, 129

Callao, 63

Cameroon, 27; Mount, 33

Canary Islands, 21-22

Carrol, Geoff, 140

Ceylon, 40

Chalmers, Alexander (father of Adams), 59-60

Chalmers, Anna (sister of Adams), 60

Chalmers, Frances Wilkins (mother of Adams), 59

Chalmers, George (uncle of Adams), 59

Cheka, 89-90

China, 6, 7, 8, 13, 38, 39, 47, 48, 49, 55, 68, 69, 91

Churchill, Marlborough, 80, 81, 85, 86

colonization, European, 9, 20, 33, 61, 118

Columbus, Christopher, 7-8, 67

communism, 85, 89, 93

Congo Français, 25, 27, 30

Congo Free State, 25, 27

conquistadors, 61

Cooper, James Fenimore, 39

Cooper, Merian C., 91, 93

Cornhill Magazine, 120

Cressy-Marcks, Violet, 12

Cuzco, 64

Dalai Lama, 42, 46, 48, 53

Dal Vera, Anne, 142, 143-144, 145, 146, 147

Damascus, 119, 120

Daughters of Sheba, 127

David, Alexandrine Borghmans

(mother), 38, 39
David, Louis Pierre (father), 38-39, 40
David-Neel, Alexandra, 36; books written by, 54, 55; death of, 55; early years of, 38-39; as hermit, 45-46; interest of, in Buddhism, 40, 42, 43, 44-45, 48, 54; relationship of, with Yongden, 37, 38, 43, 44, 45, 46, 47, 48, 49, 51, 52, 53, 54; Sanskrit studied by, 40, 41; Tibetan studied by, 43, 49, 53; travels of, in China, 13, 47-48, 49; travels of, in India, 13, 40, 41-42, 46, 53; travels of, in Tibet, 13, 37-38, 43, 44, 46, 51-53, 54, 55
Dennett, R. E., 25
dogsled, 134, 135, 136, 137, 138, 139
Drake, Francis, 8
Druze tribe, 120

Earhart, Amelia, 72
Effik tribe, 30
Eleanor of Aquitaine (queen of France), 8-9
Elizabeth I (queen of England), 8
Endurance, 134-135
Eskimos, 105, 106
Explorers Club (New York), 9

Fang tribe, 30-31, 32-33
Ferdinand (king of Spain), 8
Fernando Po, 29
fetishism, 25, 27, 29
The Fiord Region of East Greenland, 111-112
fjords, 105, 106, 107, 108, 109
Fraenkel Land, 110
Franz Josef Fjord, 105, 108, 109
Franz Josef Land, 100

Freetown, 23-24

Germany, 55, 85, 112; Harrison in, 13, 75-76, 80, 81, 82-85, 86, 90, 93
Gibson, Margaret Smith, 11-12
Giller, Sue, 142, 143-144, 145, 146, 147
Global Positioning System (GPS), 144, 147
Goodenough, William, 123-124
Grass, 93
Greenland, 99, 103, 112, 113, 142; Boyd in, 14, 95-96, 105-107, 108-111, 112
Grosvenor, Gilbert, 66
Günther, Albert Charles, 28-29, 30

Hadhramaut, Wadi, 124, 125, 126, 127, 128
Harper's Magazine, 69
Harriet Chalmers Adams Memorial Endowment Fund, 73
Harrison, Marguerite Baker: books written by, 80, 91; death of, 93; early years of, 76-77; and founding of Society of Woman Geographers, 13, 93; imprisonment of, 13, 89-91; as journalist, 74, 75, 78-79, 82, 84, 85, 86, 88, 89, 91; as spy, 13, 74, 76, 79-84, 86-91; travels of, in Germany, 13, 75-76, 81, 82-85, 86, 90, 93; travels of, in Middle East, 91-93; travels of, in Russia, 13, 85-91
Harrison, Thomas Bullitt (first husband), 77, 78
Harrison II, Thomas Bullitt (son), 78, 82, 85, 86
Himalayas, 9, 43

Hobby, 100, 102, 104
Hugo, Victor, 38

Ibibio tribe, 30
Igbo tribe, 30
Ikwan al-Hurriyah. *See*
  Brotherhood of Freedom
imam (ruler of Yemen), 124-
  125, 128, 129
Incas, 61, 64, 65, 68
India, 10, 12, 13, 39, 40, 41, 42,
  46, 47, 53, 131
Introduction to the Study of Fishes,
  28-29
Iraq, 121
Isabella (queen of Spain), 8

Jan Mayen Island, 108, 112
Japan, 10, 39, 47, 55, 69, 91

Karlin, Anna, 87
Kathiri tribe, 124
Kent, Frank, 78, 82, 86
King Oscar Fjord, 105, 108
Kingsley, Charles (brother), 18,
  22, 28, 29
Kingsley, Charles (uncle), 28
Kingsley, George (father), 18,
  21
Kingsley, Mary: books written
  by, 29, 32, 34-35; in Canary
  Islands, 21-22; as celebrity,
  33, 34, 35; death of, 35; early
  years of, 18, 19, 21; Fang
  tribe studied by, 31, 32-33;
  fetishism studied by, 25, 27,
  29; fish specimens collected
  by, 28-29, 30, 34; travels of,
  in Africa, 13, 16, 17-18, 20-
  21, 22-27, 29-33
Kingsley, Mary Bailey (mother),
  18-19, 21
Kumbum, 48

Lagos, 23, 24-25

Lansing, Alfred, 134
Latin America, 59, 61; Adams
  in, 13, 56, 58-59, 60, 63-65,
  67, 70
Lebanon, 118
Lenin, Vladimir, 85-86, 89
Lewis, Agnes Smith, 11-12
Lhasa, 37, 38, 47, 48, 50, 52, 53,
  54
Lima, 63
Lubianka Prison, 89, 90, 91

Macdonald, David, 53
McKerrow, Bob, 138
McKinley, Mount, 135
McMurdo Station, 149
Maillart, Ella, 12
Malaysia, 11, 69
Mantell, Bob, 138
Marooned in Moscow, 91
Mary Kingsley Society of West
  Africa, 35
Mazuchelli, Elizabeth Sarah, 9
Middle East, 9, 91-92, 115, 118;
  Stark in, 13, 115-116, 118-
  123, 124-129, 131
Military Intelligence Division
  (MID), U.S. Army, 76, 80,
  81, 84, 90
The Minaret of Djam, 130
monasteries, Buddhist, 43, 44,
  46, 47, 48
Mongolia, 49, 68, 91
Moor, 35
Moscow, 87, 88, 89
Murphy, Dervla, 12

National Geographic, 66, 73, 141
National Geographic Society,
  66, 71, 141
Native Americans, 67-68, 70
Nazis, 85
Neel, Philippe-François
  (husband of David-Neel), 40-
  41

New York Times, 96
Nigeria, 27, 29
Nile River, 9
Nobile, Umberto, 103, 104
North Pole, 13, 95, 100, 101,
103, 113, 135, 136, 139;
reached by Bancroft, 14, 132,
134, 140, 145
Northwest Territories, 136,
137, 142
Norway, 99, 103, 104, 107, 108,
112

The Odyssey, 7
Ogooué River, 30, 31
Ollantaytambo, 64, 65
Ottoman Empire, 118

Panchen Lama, 46, 48
Paris Peace Conference, 81, 84
Peary, Robert, 136
Peking, 47
Perowne, Stewart (husband of
Stark), 130
Persia, 11, 92, 131
Peru, 58, 63, 64, 67, 73
Philby, Harry St. John, 127
photogrammetry, 106, 112
Poland, 86, 87
Polo, Marco, 6, 7, 8
Potala, 53, 54
Pygmy tribes, 12

Qu'aiti tribe, 124
Quechua Indians, 64, 68
Queen Maud Land, 149

Remboué River, 30, 32
Ross Ice Shelf, 149, 150
Royal Geographical Society, 9,
11, 70, 123, 124
Russia, 55; Harrison in, 13, 85-
91; revolution in, 85

Samten Dzong, 55

Sanskrit, 40, 41
Schoedsack, Earnest "Shorty,"
92, 93
Schurke, Paul, 137, 140
Seiyun, 125
Shabwa, 124, 125, 126, 127
Shackleton, Ernest, 134
Siberia, 9, 91
Sierra Leone, 23, 25
Sikkim, 42, 43, 44, 45
silk road, 6
Society of Woman
Geographers, 13, 71, 72, 73,
93
Sorby, Sunniva, 142, 143-145,
146, 147
The Southern Gates of Arabia,
127
South Pole, 141; reached by
Bancroft, 14, 15, 132, 145,
146, 147, 149, 151
Spitsbergen, 99-100
Stark, Flora (mother), 116, 117
Stark, Freya: Arabic studied by,
13, 118, 119, 120, 125;
awards and honors of, 123,
130; death of, 131; early years
of, 116-117; search of, for
Shabwa, 124-127; travels of,
in Middle East, 13, 115-116,
118-123, 124-129, 131; work
of, for British government
during World War II, 127-
129; as writer, 13, 114, 116,
120, 124, 127, 130
Stark, Robert (father), 116
Stark, Vera (sister), 116
Steger, Will, 135-136, 139, 140
Steger International Polar
Expedition, 134, 135-140
Syria, 11, 119

theosophy, 40
There's Always Tomorrow, 80
Tibet, 42, 46-47, 54; David-

Neel in, 13, 37-38, 43, 44, 46, 48, 51-53, 54, 55
Tigris and Euphrates Rivers, 121
Travels in West Africa, 34
Trotsky, Leon, 89
Troy, 7
Tulku, Sidkeong, 42-43
Turkey, 92, 130
Two Trips to Gorilla Land, 20

Unfinished Tales from a Russian Prison, 91

The Valley of the Assassins, 124
vampire bats, 58, 59
Verne, Jules, 39
Versailles, Treaty of, 84-85
Veslekari, 95, 104, 105, 108, 109, 111
von Sass Baker, Florence, 9

Weber, Richard, 140
West Africa. *See* Africa
West African Studies, 35
Wood, Walter A., 106, 108, 113
World War I, 13, 44, 69-70, 75, 78-79, 81, 99, 117
World War II, 85, 93, 112, 127, 129, 130

Yemen, 124-125, 127, 128, 129
Yongden, 37, 38, 43, 44, 45, 46, 47, 48, 49, 51, 52, 53, 54
yourexpedition, 147

ABOUT THE AUTHOR

JACQUELINE McLEAN earned a doctorate in English literature from New York University in 1996. She writes frequently for young adults and children; her passions include extraordinary women's stories, travel, and the experience of other cultures. She is the author of The Oliver Press book *Women With Wings*, as well as *Grace from China*, a young-adult novel about international adoption. McLean currently teaches in the English department at Texas Tech University. She and the poet William Wenthe live in West Texas with their corgi, Edward, and cats, Spanky and Zero.

Photo Credits

Photographs courtesy of: cover, pp. 132, 143, 146, 148, 151, yourexpedition.com; pp. 6, 20, 24, 25, 83, 114, 128, Hulton/Archive by Getty Images; pp. 10, 11, 12, 56, 65, 68, 79, 81, 88, 94, 103, 119, 121, back cover, Library of Congress; pp. 14 (from *The Coast of Northeast Greenland* by Louise Arner Boyd, by permission of the American Geographical Society), 106, 107, 110 (from *The Coast of Northeast Greenland* by Louise Arner Boyd, by permission of the American Geographical Society), The American Geographical Society Collection, University of Wisconsin-Milwaukee Library; p. 16, Liverpool Record Office and Local Studies Department; p. 28, National Portrait Gallery, London; p. 31, Mary Evans Picture Library; pp. 32, 34, *Travels in West Africa* by Mary Kingsley; pp. 36, 41, 43, 44, 45, 47, 52, 54, Fondation Alexandra David-Neel; pp. 61, 67, 69, Stockton-San Joaquin County Public Library; pp. 72, 74, 92, The Society of Woman Geographers; pp. 98, 101, 109, Marin History Museum; pp. 122, 126, 129, The Middle East Centre, St. Antony's College, Oxford; p. 137, Will Steger; p. 140, Jim Gaspirini.